What they're sayin
GETTING THE BEST SCORE
FOR YOUR FILM

"David Bell has written a comprehensive account of everything a director and producer should know to obtain a first-rate film score. He has much to say about the collaboration between director and composer and the pitfalls to avoid in what can be an exciting creative relationship. The book contains a wealth of information covering the technical, artistic, and budgetary aspects of film scoring and should be read by anyone who wants to direct or produce a film in Hollywood."

— John Addison, composer,
Tom Jones, Sleuth

"David Bell champions the pure art of scoring, as typified by the 'Golden Days of Hollywood,' while squarely dealing with the contemporary realities of film music in the '90s. Filmmakers and future filmmakers alike . . . read this book so that we can all be 'reading from the same page of the playbook.'"

— Paul Broucek, Music Supervisor,
Klean/Broucek Music

"This book is the ideal 'weekend read' for producers, associate producers, production accountants, directors and virtually anyone who comes in contact with music for the film and television industry. In times of restricted budgets, it becomes increasingly important for everyone in our industry to get the most 'bang for the buck.' This is the only book I know that facilitates that end where music is concerned."

— Richard R. Bellis, Emmy-winning
composer, President of The Society
of Composers and Lyricists

"An invaluable and informative guide to the process of scoring films."

— Elmer Bernstein, composer,
To Kill a Mockingbird, Rambling Rose

"In this excellent book, David Bell outlines the production of the music score and conveys superbly, in direct and simple language, ways in which to facilitate and maximize the exciting and creative collaboration between the director and the composer, providing astute insights into the processes by which the director can with ease and confidence realize his vision of the music score. Essential reading for every filmmaker."

— Trevor Jones, composer,
Mississippi Burning, Cliffhanger

"David Bell has written a clear, concise, and detailed book on the business and art of film scoring in the '90s."

— Jay Roewe, Vice President of Production,
HBO Pictures

"The creator of movie music delivers the art most difficult for the average producer to understand in its formative stages. Here's a fine guide through that jungle."

— Buck Houghton, producer,
The Twilight Zone, author
of *What a Producer Does*

". . . a successful composer, orchestrator, and seminar speaker . . . David Bell is certainly knowledgeable about his material."

— Bruce Broughton, composer,
Silverado, The Presidio

"The craft of composing music for film goes beyond merely writing good music. David Bell possesses the experience and skills that make him both a consummate professional and a superb composer."

— Richard S. Kaufman, Vice President
of Music for MGM

Getting the Best SCORE for Your Film

Getting the Best SCORE for Your Film

A Filmmakers' Guide to Music Scoring

David Bell

SILMAN-JAMES PRESS
Los Angeles

First edition

10 9 8 7 6 5 4 3

Library of Congress Cataloging-in-Publication Data

Bell, David A.
Getting the best score for your film ; a filmmakers' guide to
music scoring / by David Bell. — 1st ed.
p.   cm.
Includes bibliographical references (p.   ).
1. Motion pictures and music. 2. Music trade—United States.
I. Title.
ML2075.B42   1994   781.5'4213—dc20   94-30604

ISBN: 1-879505-20-7

Cover design by Heidi Frieder
Printed in the United States of America

Silman-James Press
1181 Angelo Drive
Beverly Hills, CA 90201

CONTENTS

INTRODUCTION

One of the greatest challenges faced by the filmmaker is dealing with the music score, yet only recently has it begun to be addressed by some film schools. Granted, various organizations occasionally offer discussions between famous composers and directors, but it is rare for anyone to speak directly with filmmakers about such basics as budget numbers, personnel involved, choosing a composer, communicating with a composer, and the time required to write and produce a score. The goal of this book is to foster a better understanding of the scoring process and the tools needed by the composer, for this will help the filmmaker communicate his/her needs so as to use time, money, and creativity most efficiently.

The power of music is such that a few notes can drastically alter a scene (for better or for worse), and the music-scoring process is an area in which filmmakers often feel that they don't have much control over the outcome. I hope this book will present enough information about the process of scoring films so that you, the filmmaker, may enjoy the collaboration with your composer and have the control you want over the soundtrack. By giving some general guidelines or "do's and don'ts," I hope that the road to the finished score will be a smooth one for all concerned. This book may not provide the answer for every situation, but at least *it serves as a point of departure for discussion between you and your composer.* As the football coach once said, "It's important we're all reading from the same page of the playbook." This book is based on my experience as a composer working in film and television and on my many conversations with filmmakers and composers.

I hope to communicate two main points with this book. The first is that the production of a good soundtrack sometimes requires assembling a veritable army of professionals. The process takes time and money (more time can often overcome a shortage of money). If filmmakers and production accountants have a good understanding of the realities of music production (many of which are beyond the composer's control), many of the unnecessary heartaches that sometimes occur during the scoring process can be eliminated.

The second is that directors and composers are artistic kin. We've been through a similar training process and have the same love for craft and artistic values. Most film composers get a genuine thrill out of the creative collaboration in film art and will do all they can to please the filmmaker; working with the composer should be an enjoyable creative collaboration of two artists in love with the project.

Within this book, I use the word "filmmaker" to refer to both the producer and the director, for the issues that follow are important to both. I also bow to the standard literary convention of using the masculine "he" or "him" when I mean "he/she" or "him/her." Music scoring terms that may be unfamiliar to you are defined in the glossary.

I want to express my appreciation to the following people for their clarification of certain details: Dennis Spiegel for songwriting issues, Paul Broucek for Music Supervisor issues, Dennis Dreith and Dan Savant for union and budget matters, and Todd Brabec, Director of Membership for ASCAP, for information pertaining to the performing rights societies. A special thanks to my friends and colleagues for reading the manuscript and making helpful suggestions: John Addison, Jon Burlingame, Ron Grant, Mark Green, Barbara Jordan, Nancy Knutsen, John Lugar, Fred Paroutaud, Bill Phillips, Rich Ruttenberg, Rayna Saslove, Bradd Saunders, Vasili Vangelos, Jack Woods, and Allen Yamashita. Thanks also to my colleagues at the Society of Composers and Lyricists, especially its former Presidents Bruce Broughton and Richard Bellis; this book is an outgrowth of seminars sponsored by that group during my tenure as seminar committee chairperson.

I'm especially grateful to Jim Fox and Gwen Feldman at Silman-James Press for their enthusiasm and guidance through this book's writing and refining process. As an avid reader, I've always wondered why authors were so effusive when expressing appreciation to publishing and editing staff. Now that I've written a book, I understand—words such as "Godsend" and "lifesaver" leap to mind.

None of this would have been possible were it not for the career-building efforts of Michael Gorfaine, Sam Schwartz, Cheryl Tiano, and the rest of the gang at The Gorfaine/Schwartz Agency.

I am forever indebted to Rayburn Wright. A great teacher and friend, his kindness and musicianship will always be an inspiration to me.

* * *

This book is dedicated to the professionals who create the film music: the musicians, copyists, music editors, scoring and dubbing mixers, techs and assistants, and, of course, my fellow composers. The disciplined professionalism and heartfelt care with which these people approach their work define the highest standards of artistry. Few composers in the history of the world have ever had their music played and recorded with such perfection; I'm honored to be a part of this magic.

David Bell, Los Angeles, 1994

1
THE FUNCTION OF UNDERSCORE

Musical underscore performs three basic functions:
    1) to play the action in a scene
    2) to play obliquely or play the subtext of a scene
    3) to play against the action in a scene.

Much like the three primary colors in painting, these three functions can be combined and manipulated to create many gradations of musical interplay.

No matter which of these functions is chosen as a primary musical direction, the best film music taps into the core emotion of a film. It moves the plot along, it enhances the cohesiveness of the drama, it reflects what's obvious on the screen or what isn't; at its best, it speaks to the deepest levels of emotion the audience is supposed to feel. Good film music becomes a character all its own, weaving itself throughout the fabric of the film.

Music and sound effects give film a third dimension. Whereas the projected image is two-dimensional and presented on the screen, the music and sound reach into the theater and embrace the audience. This general concept is important to understand when deciding how music will function in your film. Also note that the art of creating a good film score is knowing when to use silence well.

PLAYING THE ACTION

This type of underscore directly reflects the obvious actions and emotions on the screen. This is the underscore of cartoons, the chases accompanied by a driving rock 'n' roll rhythm, or the suspense music that stalks the murderer as he stalks his victim.

Artful examples of playing the action on the screen are the *Star Wars* and *Raiders of the Lost Ark* adventure scores of John Williams and the suspense scores of Bernard Herrmann. In *Psycho*, Herrmann's famous shrieking, screaming strings as the shower curtain is yanked back and the stabbing commences plays the action and victim's feelings as literally as possible, yet it's brilliant underscoring that will frighten audiences for generations. When the film and the music are both finely crafted, there's nothing wrong with playing the action directly (although one is always looking to tap into deeper dramatic moments whenever possible).

Playing the action becomes uninteresting when the scripted characters, acting, and filmmaking are one-dimensional, as is common in the average low-budget action/exploitation film. Typically, these types of films are married to a very average underscore (often poorly written rock 'n' roll) that simply exaggerates the one-dimensional quality of the project. A well-composed score can help bring these films to a slightly higher level, but there are limits to this (see "What Film Music Can't Do" at the end of this chapter). If deep, multi-dimensional dramatic content doesn't exist somewhere within the film, the music can't fabricate it.

The above paragraph in no way implies that rock 'n' roll underscore is a negative thing. Many of James Newton Howard's scores are rooted in rock 'n' roll and are extremely well-crafted. His score for *The Fugitive* was particularly stunning because music was used in most of the film. For Howard (and the filmmakers) to keep the tension at a consistently high level throughout was a particularly daunting challenge, and they pulled it off magnificently. By combining a rock 'n' roll groove with a symphonic orchestra, he had a huge musical color palette with which to work; the constant changing of instrumental colors is what allowed him to sustain a groove for such long periods of time. Contrast this score to that of the typical exploitation film, where the drum beat and instrumental colors remain fairly constant, and you'll quickly see the difference between good underscore and not-so-good underscore.

It's difficult to make general rules about music, but if you listen to a few well-crafted music scores (the four mentioned above are excellent examples), you'll find that one of the main components of high-quality music is this constant (and frequent) changing of instrumental colors within a specific palette: large ensemble to small (full orchestra to solos or duets), very busy to very simple, etc. This technique is never more important than when playing the action directly. The compositional craft and adequate time (variety requires thought) and budget must exist for this to happen, however.

Chase scenes are a good example of grappling with the creative choices of whether or not to play the action directly. With some chases—those with true dramatic substance and purpose—it's possible to try a more artful, unusual approach such as playing it sparsely or even playing against the chase with slow music (say a beautiful opera aria). Sometimes no music at all is the best choice—Steve McQueen's famous car chase through San Francisco in *Bullitt* had no underscore. However, trying these same artful approaches with the typical, gratuitous chase scene will merely make it look worse. The deeper dramatic level or subtext must exist within the content of the scene for the unusual musical choice to work.

PLAYING OBLIQUELY OR PLAYING THE SUBTEXT

This type of underscore plays to a greater depth of character or drama than is immediately apparent on the screen. For instance, Jerry Goldsmith's score to *Patton* was composed of three basic elements: (1) the military march, (2) the echoing trumpet figure, and (3) the cathedral organ chorale. The first reflected the obvious character component of Patton, the warrior. The second and third plumbed the depths of his character. The haunting trumpet-echo figure signified Patton's deep belief that he had been reincarnated several times throughout history (the trumpet notes echo into the past), and the cathedral organ signified his deep religious convictions. The complexity of the character was reflected in one of the greatest scores in the history of film. This level of composing doesn't happen by accident nor does it happen overnight; it is due to the composer and director having good communication and plenty of time to research and discuss ideas.

For an example of film music playing the subtext of a scene, consider this: Handsome Guy is painting a house on a hot summer day (sweaty, glistening, bare torso, of course) and Pretty Girl acquaintance walks up. They talk about house painting in breathy tones ("ooh, that paint goes on so smo-o-o-othly"), all the while making sexy goo-goo eyes and suggestive smiles at each other. Naturally, the conversation isn't really about painting, it's about sex. Most likely, the music would reflect that by being sexy and steamy in character.

An oblique score might be somewhat neutral in character. This type of music tells the audience that something more is occuring in a scene than that which is obvious, but doesn't "telegraph" the real meaning. This tends to bring the audience into the film; they become more involved as they wonder "what's happening next?" or "what does this really mean?" Too often, composers and film-makers make musical choices that spoon-feed so much obvious information to audiences that we bore them. It's our job to bring the viewer into the film and make the viewer curious, and music can accomplish that very effectively. Even if the action on the screen *is* meant to be obvious, a rather murky, uncertain music cue can keep the audience a little off balance so that they don't get too confident and predict the outcome. Mark Isham did this very well in films such as *Trouble in Mind*, *The Moderns*, and *Mrs. Soffel*.

PLAYING AGAINST THE ACTION

This type of musical underscore plays completely opposite the action on the screen. Because of its seeming incongruity, it is star-tling and very effective as it plays the very deepest truth of the drama. A prime example of this is John Williams' score to *Jaws*. Many of the early underwater shots we see from the shark's point of view are beautiful and serene; the only element that tells us this is really a place of great danger is the low, pulsating music.

Ennio Morricone's score to *The Mission* also does this excep-tionally well. Note how the tender, peaceful vocal chorale plays against the massacre scene and is literally a requiem for all of the victims of violence and greed in the film. At the climax of the massacre when Mendoza (Robert DeNiro) and Gabriel (Jeremy Irons) die, the sad, haunting oboe solo pierces through the ter-rible violence on the screen and cuts directly through to the soul of the viewer.

This is the same principle that was behind the sad string elegy (Samuel Barber's *Adagio for Strings*) used so effectively playing against the images of the machines of war in the opening sequence of the film *Platoon*.

Another good example of this was Francis Ford Coppola's musical choice for the end of *The Godfather*, as Michael Corleone has his enemies murdered while he's attending a baby christening in the church. Although Coppola intercuts between the christening and the murders, the church organ and priest's recitation of the Latin service continue throughout, serving as underscore to the violent killings.

WHAT FILM MUSIC CAN'T DO

A famous story, which I've heard attributed to Bernard Herrmann, goes like this: A distressed director pleaded with Herrmann to screen his very flawed film, hoping that the master composer could fix it with a brilliant score. After the screening, the director eagerly approached Herrmann and asked, "Well? Can you save it?" to which Herrmann supposedly replied, "I can dress it up, but I can't bring it back to life." Certainly, music can help weak scenes, and certainly Herrmann could have been more diplomatic, but the story illustrates a point about the limitations of music.

"Save the scene" music is the most difficult to write—the scene is usually dying because it lacks focused dramatic content; it doesn't give the composer anything on which to hang his musical hat. In these cases, musical "wallpaper" is often written and placed in the scene to hide the blemishes. This can become a habit, and pretty soon lots of "wallpaper" music gets stuffed into lots of scenes and we find ourselves in musical/dramatic quicksand. Although music may help the occasional weak scene a bit by giving the perception of speeding it up, too much incorrect use of music will probably do more damage to the film than if it hadn't been used at all.

This creative choice usually occurs during the construction of the temp track or in the spotting session as the filmmaker and composer decide where the music should be placed within the body of the film. However, I experienced an unusual variation on this phenomenon after completing the score for a motion picture. Before and during the composing of this score, the filmmakers and

I had many discussions about the musical structure in the film—the themes and their variations were spotted (placed) carefully. However, the filmmakers loved the final score so much that they made multiple copies of their favorite cues and added music throughout the film. Although I was flattered by their enthusiasm for my work, packing the film with music made the score too repetitive and, in my opinion, damaged the structure of the film.

The bottom line: By putting music in places where it doesn't have a strong, focused function, the effectiveness of the music in places where it does belong is diluted. Ideally, *music should only be in the film when there is a clear dramatic reason for its existence.*

2
CHOOSING THE COMPOSER

WHEN TO HIRE THE COMPOSER

As soon as possible.

The composer needs time to discuss musical concepts with the filmmaker; study the characters, their surroundings, and period in history; think of a general musical vocabulary and themes; and begin planning the logistics of producing the score. Just as the actors and filmmakers normally have time to think about, discuss, research, and shape the character of the roles to be played, the composer and director should have plenty of time to do the same for the character of the music.

Some composers like to be involved before the shoot so that they can be privy to the filmmaker's thought processes from the beginning and pick up clues about his dramatic/musical vision. Others prefer to be brought in during the rough cut—by this time, the film may have changed quite a bit from the script and the filmmaker's pre-shoot vision. In this latter case, the composer enters the postproduction process with a fresh perspective that hasn't been colored by months of discussion; this can be beneficial.

If prescore is required, hire the composer two or three months before shooting begins so that the prerecorded song or dance music can be incorporated into the shooting schedule (not forgetting, of course, that it will then take a certain amount of time for on-screen dances/songs to be choreographed and rehearsed to that prescore). When using prescore music, there *must* be a person with musical training (music editor and/or music supervisor) on the set during shooting to be sure that the technical matters of synching playback and film are done correctly and to ensure that

the on-screen musicians faking to the prerecorded music are han-
dling the instruments realistically. If this isn't coordinated properly,
it can lead to later editorial problems that may be insurmountable.

If the composer is involved during the rough cut, he can help
with pacing in certain spots. Sometimes filmmakers are uneasy
with silence—lots of film running by with no dialogue or sound
effects can be unnerving, and some strong musical moments can
get shortchanged when these silences are edited out. The composer can reassure the filmmaker that holding on a certain shot
for three or four more seconds will allow the music to make a
stronger statement.

For instance, visualize the last cut of a final scene: a lingering
close-up on the tearful face of a young girl gazing sadly as her
soldier-boyfriend's train leaves the station on the way to war—fade
to black. Let's say that the composer chooses to place a warm, full,
final chord on this last cut. The resonance of one long, warm chord
(with no moving notes) goes through the following stages: gentle
beginning, swell, holding of full resonance, slow diminishing in
volume, cutoff, full reverberation, followed by a bit of silent film
at the end of the fade.* A single chord such as this could take as
much as ten to fifteen seconds to make its full statement, yet this
same cut played in silence during the editing process may seem
much too long. It's important to linger on such moments and it
may be helpful to consult with your composer, who should have
a good sense of musical sound properties and the time they require to make their most powerful impact.

The rough cut is a good time to discuss general musical concepts. The filmmaker and composer can work out themes and play
many different styles of music with the film to see what does and
doesn't work. Most composers have a large collection of their own
music plus recordings of other film scores that are usually at your
disposal. If you temp track** the film, having the composer help
you and the music editor with it can be a good way to communicate your musical vision. Whenever possible, temp track with your

---

* One of the best tips I ever received as a young orchestra conductor was this: When
giving the final cutoff at the end of a piece of music, don't just wait for the sound to
end, but keep the arms raised and allow the silence to grow . . .
** A temporary music soundtrack built from pre-existing film scores is usually constructed for the purpose of studio and test screenings.

composer's tape or CD library of his own music so that his stylistic imprint is in the temp rather than that of another composer.

The bottom line is, *give the composer as much time as possible.* The more time you and the composer have to get acquainted, the better you'll communicate and the better he will be able to realize your creative vision. A rule of thumb is to plan on a composer writing two or three minutes of good, finished music per day (*after* the main themes have been approved and the picture is locked and spotted). The composer then needs additional time for meetings with the filmmaker to discuss and preview music cues on piano or synthesizer, book the recording stage, book the scoring mixer, plan the size of the orchestra to fit the budget, and determine how that relates to the time needed to record the required number of minutes of music, plus many other logistical details.

After the picture is locked, four to six weeks is the minimum amount of time needed to compose the score for a feature film, two to three weeks for a television movie, and a week to ten days for a one-hour episode of television. These schedules can vary slightly depending on the complexity of the music, amount of time discussing/previewing cues with the filmmaker, instrumentation, amount of music, etc.

Having plenty of time during the postproduction scoring process is especially important when the budget is skimpy. The more time the composer has, the bigger musical bang you'll get for your buck: He can plan the composing and recording sessions to utilize musicians and stage time most efficiently, do his own orchestration, etc.

Waiting until the picture is locked to hire a composer means less time for in-depth discussions between the composer and filmmaker, less time for fine-tuning themes, and so forth. When working on a tight deadline, the composer is compelled to write down the first musical idea that comes to mind; there isn't time to explore other, perhaps better, creative possibilities.

Hiring the composer at an early date won't cost more money, it will only result in a better score.

HOW TO HIRE THE COMPOSER

- pre-existing personal relationships
- listening to demo tapes/CDs
- checking list of credits
- good chemistry in interview
- personal recommendation of other filmmakers, music supervisors, film editors, and music editors

Pre-existing personal relationships

Ideally, the relationship between filmmaker and composer is one of creative intimacy. The music is addressing the heart and soul of the film and, when a composer and filmmaker have a long-standing relationship, the composer is often better able to touch dramatic points that have become unspoken understandings. Some prime examples of long-term composer/director relationships are those of John Williams/Steven Spielberg and Henry Mancini/Blake Edwards. The films and scores that these teams produced have wonderful creative chemistry that probably could only have been achieved through that long-term relationship/understanding.

Showing loyalty to a composer is rewarded in kind by that composer's strong committment to you and your work—this can pay enormous dividends. When an artist feels relaxed and secure in a relationship, he usually produces better work because his attention is on creating music, not on the production-office politics or other distractions. Sometimes the filmmaker may want a bit of variety in his choice of musical collaborators; this is especially true when he's used the same composer for all 100-plus episodes of a television series. Variety can be achieved by alternating episodes or projects between two or three composers. Even if you decide to use a different composer once in a while, take a few minutes to call the composer with whom you've established a relationship and reassure him that he's not being fired, that you liked his last score and will work with him again in the future, but at this time you feel like trying a bit of compositional variety. He'll understand; after all, composers don't always use the same musicians for every score they write. You'll get extra effort from the composer through loyalty, appreciation, and basic courtesy.

Listening to demo tapes

In listening and sorting through these tapes, the main objective is to *find music that is interesting to you, even though it may be a different style than you are looking for.* Many filmmakers listen to demo tapes/CDs to find music that will already fit their film stylistically. This is safe, but not necessarily the best way to get a unique, interesting, and original score for your project; by doing this, you're essentially asking the composer to rewrite a score that he penned for another movie.

The term "interesting" as used above is problematic, and I use it conditionally. Very noticeable music that is interesting to listen to is not necessarily good film music. Good film music is sometimes inherently boring to listen to, for it isn't intended to stand on its own; it's designed to service the film and often be unobtrusive. Search for music that clearly defines a mood, something that is not generic. Every composer demo tape/CD will have large, bombastic music cues on it, but listen carefully to the subtle cues and try to imagine how they would work under dialogue. Listen for unpredictability in the music; the composer who tosses in the occasional unusual note or rhythm has a more unique and interesting approach.

Try to avoid "pigeonholing" composers. Most professional film composers are very versatile and are trained to write in all styles. Associating a composer with one style is a disservice to your film; it excludes many exciting possibilities of "cross-casting" a composer. Although John Williams had done fifty to sixty films of varied musical styles before he began composing the *Star Wars* trilogy, I spoke to many producers in the early- and mid-1980s who were convinced that adventure music was all he could write. Thankfully, some filmmakers saw beyond that and hired him to write the music for such films as *The Accidental Tourist, The Witches of Eastwick, Born on the Fourth of July*, and *JFK*, which represent film music at its very best.

You may also have a friend who has had extensive musical training help you listen to some of the tapes (blindly, without seeing names or film titles). This could be a way of weeding out the charlatans; i.e., those whose synthesizers produce all the latest sounds but who don't know how to use them in a musical way. Perhaps you know a studio musician; mention the names of a few composers who are in the "finals" of your selection process and get their reaction. Most studio musicians love being a part of the film industry and enjoy playing film music that is well-written and conducted; they know who's good and who's not. A qualified music supervisor can be extremely helpful during this filtering process.

I recommend that the filmmaker lock himself away in a room, with no distractions, and spend short sessions (forty to fifty minutes or eight to ten tapes/CDs is my limit) listening to a few minutes of each demo tape. Try to use the same playback system and room for all your listening sessions; the sound system should be of good quality. I don't recommend listening to tapes while driving in a car. The sounds made by your car, the wind, and other traffic noise will wash out approximately 50% of the music and orchestration. Some of the tapes will be difficult to sit through, but sometimes it's valuable to experience bad art so that you can better define good art.

When requesting demo tapes, do all you can to give the composers or their agents
- an accurate description of the film
- the mood or type of music you're seeking
- the music budget
- the time schedule
- the instrumentation (synthesized or orchestral)
- the names of pre-existing scores that you feel are stylistically appropriate for your film.

It's a tremendous help for the composer to read a script before assembling a demo tape/CD.

Anyone who has made a film or video in recent years that has had the slightest mention in a trade paper or magazine during production has probably been inundated with demo tapes/CDs from composers and composer agents. Tapes/CDs arrive from established composers as well as from the hundreds of young, recently arrived composers (a huge influx since the mid-1980s). For the past couple decades, the synthesizer has been a wonderful new color for composers to use in their work. In recent years, synthesizer/sampler techonology has grown in sophistication and accessibility yet dropped in price. This dazzling push-button technology

with its preprogrammed sounds makes it possible for almost anyone to call himself a composer. Keep in mind that receiving a
demo tape/CD with the latest hip sounds produced on a synthesizer does not mean that you're dealing with a good film composer.

On rare occasions, filmmakers ask composers to submit video
excerpts of their work. Based on personal experience and conversations with other composers, I generally advise against that
practice. When seeing a piece of film, filmmakers naturally focus
on the writing, acting, directing, cinematography, etc., and their
reaction to these elements will no doubt color their perception of
the music. For instance, the lead actor in a scene submitted by the
composer may be someone whose work the filmmaker dislikes—
this can put the composer up to bat with one strike against him
at the outset.

Checking list of credits

Film music is an art that requires more knowledge than just
writing good music. The music must work dramatically, it must
function well under dialogue and sound effects, and it must fit the
timing of the picture—all three of which require experience. The
composer must match film and music within a tolerance of 2/10
of a second to a constant (the speed of the film projection) and
still know how to give the music an artful ebb and flow. He must
not only fit the music as he writes, but also be able to conduct
well enough to ensure the performance of the musicians matches
the film (although some composers hire conductors so that they
can sit in the recording booth and monitor the mix). The composer
must also know how to communicate with the filmmaker during
the composing process and at the recording session to avoid costly
delays.

A "comfort" factor is also involved here—hiring a composer
whose credits reflect work in films of a similar type to your own
is reassuring. This is certainly safe, but sometimes pushing the
boundaries of that comfort factor can result in an unusual and
exciting score.

If you're making a feature film, don't automatically shy away
from a composer whose credits are primarily in television. A good
deal of "crossover" work is being done, and the lines drawn between feature and television composers are not so sharp now. The

techniques, musicians hired, and artistic disciplines of television and feature-film music are identical. In fact, music appearing on television is often more adventurous because the extremely high budgets of feature films in recent years have created an esthetic conservatism; the tendency is to play it safe and predictable when so much money is at stake. It's been a long time since we've heard truly daring feature film music such as John Corigliano's score to *Altered States* or Jerry Goldsmith's *Planet of the Apes*.

A composer who has experience in television can be especially valuable to the low- and medium-budget film. By working with the restricted budgets and deadlines in television, he has learned to be extremely efficient with his use of time in the recording session, and he knows how to write and orchestrate well for an ensemble of limited size as well as for the large orchestra. Remember that many of today's top feature-film composers worked in television for years (many of those adventuresome scores on the original *Twilight Zone* series were written by Jerry Goldsmith).

Good chemistry in interview

Once you've whittled down those dozens of demo tapes/CDs to a couple of composers, invite them in for a meeting.

Much of the previous section on pre-existing personal relationships covers this area of personal chemistry; it may seem somewhat self-explanatory on the surface, but by "good chemistry," I don't necessarily mean to hire the composer with the funniest repartee. By nature, some composers are introverted—they spend a lot of time alone studying famous concert works and film scores, listening to CDs, composing, thinking, reading, etc.—activities that generally are not conducive to building dazzling conversation/ interview skills. A few other composers have great business acumen and are terrific salespeople, but the best score for your film may come from the quiet, studious composer. He may be the one who, by studying your film and your vision in his thoughtful manner, will musically tap into the true heart and soul of your project.

Personal recommendations of other filmmakers, music supervisors, film editors, and music editors

Check around with as many people as you can; find the composer who has a reputation for putting his all into creating a score. Look for the composer who feels passionately about his art, his profession—and, consequently, your film. For instance, if you find that a composer you're thinking of hiring uses ghostwriters or tiptoes around the issue of plagiarism, this is probably a good indication that the passion for his craft and your film isn't there. The job may be adequate, but the score will probably not convey the feeling that "blood, sweat, and tears" were shed for your project.

You can also find out how efficient this composer is on the scoring stage. Will he get you the biggest bang for your dollar? Does he treat the people around him (musicians, scoring mixers, etc.) with courtesy to get the best performance out of them? Is he one who keeps within deadlines? For instance, handing in his scores at the last minute to copyists and music editors makes it more likely that these people will make errors in copying the parts or in programming computer synch to studio recording and playback equipment, thereby wasting time on the recording stage and creating an atmosphere of frustration for everyone in the room. Is he honest? If the composer is operating on a package deal (see Chapter 14 on "Package Deals"), will he pocket most of the money or take just his fair share and use the appropriate amount to get you the best score possible? Fellow filmmakers and your music supervisor will be good resources for finding the answers to these questions.

THE POP/ROCK RECORDING ARTIST AS FILM COMPOSER

In the past, film studios had an informal apprenticeship system.* The studio music supervisors/directors were trained musicians (often composers themselves) who kept close control over which composers/orchestrators worked on the studio's pictures and in

---

* The breakdown of this semi-organized apprenticeship program at the studios is not in Hollywood's long-term interests; the best training for tomorrow's film composers is to be able to work steadily and hear their compositions and orchestrations performed on a regular basis. In recent years, a few university music departments and organizations such as ASCAP and BMI have begun to provide classes in film scoring for young composers to take up some of the slack created when the major studios' apprenticeship systems died out, but these aren't nearly enough.

what capacity. For young composers, an apprenticeship of orchestrating and arranging was sometimes rewarded with a "break" at composing televison episodes or "B" movies, with possible future work on more prestigious feature films. This is the way most of today's great film composers—such as John Williams, Jerry Goldsmith, Elmer Bernstein, and Henry Mancini—made it to the top. These gentlemen write the notes themselves and are highly respected by their colleagues for both their dramatic and musical craft. In recent years, this protective screening process has weakened, and many young "instant composers" or pop/rock artists who aren't qualified by training or experience to be underscore composers are being hired to write the music for big films.

You may love a new hit recording by a pop/rock recording artist, or the sound a rock band gets in a nightclub, but these artists may not be qualified to create a good musical underscore.* The equivalent would be hiring a fashion photographer to be a cinematographer, something that wouldn't make sense; although photographers and cinematographers both work with 35mm film, cameras, and lenses, the disciplines are not interchangeable. The same is true for underscore composers and pop/rock concert artists. It requires a different kind of experience to learn the art of writing musical underscore around dialogue and sound effects.

In certain situations, you might feel that it's imperative to hire a pop/rock artist who has little or no film experience to compose your score. Just be aware that risks and tradeoffs are involved.

When hiring a pop/rock artist to write an orchestral score, chances are that he'll be a "hummer." The hummer's compositional talent is limited to humming or playing a simple tune; it's pretty certain that 95% of the music will actually be written by a ghostwriter/orchestrator, which can result in a rather generic sound. It's not enough to plink a one-finger tune on the piano, then let an orchestrator decide which instrument(s) should play it; the best melodies are composed with specific instruments or synthesizer/acoustic colors in mind. For instance, the haunting trumpet solos

---

* Some jazz/pop/rock artists—such as James Newton Howard and Dave Grusin—started their film-scoring careers with low-budget motion pictures and learned the craft from the bottom up; I'm not referring to them in this section. Here, I'm referring to those who are plucked from the concert stage and immediately handed big-budget films.

throughout John Williams' score for *Born on the Fourth of July* were conceived for that instrument; the intervals, tempo, register and rhythms would not have the same dramatic impact if played on another instrument. True composing is the art of conceiving the complete vision of instrumentation, melody, harmony, counterpoint, and orchestration in the brain's inner ear and being able to write down the detailed components on paper or computer.

The use of a pop/rock recording artist as an underscore composer has other drawbacks as well. A specific, efficient system of putting music to film has evolved over the past few decades, and the pop/rock artist probably hasn't learned that system. It usually takes the pop/rock artist much longer than normal to make the music fit the picture properly in the recording session because they're learning the craft by trial and error. Having a large 90-piece orchestra on the clock while the pop/rock artist is learning the basics of music timings, making quick musical/orchestration changes on the recording stage, etc., is an expensive proposition. This makes everyone's life more difficult: the music editors (who must either teach the artist the current system or invent a new system for him), the copyists, scoring mixers, etc. And last, but not least, is the experience needed to know how to communicate with the filmmaker. Trying to translate the thoughts of a visual person (the filmmaker) into the aural vocabulary of the composer is always a challenge for both.*

Below are ways to attach the pop/rock artist's name to your project, yet minimize the risk of cost overruns and jeopardizing the quality of the underscore.

Most film composers are trained to be able to write in all musical styles, so if you like a particular pop/rock artist, one way of incorporating that style to your film score is to ask your composer to create an underscore that has the flavor of that artist.

---

* This is not just an issue with pop/rock artists. There have been many instances in the past where Hollywood's attempts to utilize the talents of famous classically trained concert composers have been unsuccessful for many of the same reasons. However, most concert composers adapt to film scoring more easily due to their formal training in orchestration and the classical music literature. Studying symphonic and operatic works has often left the concert composer better equipped to compose alongside action, under dialogue, and understand how dramatic structure unfolds over a long period of time (such as a two-hour movie).

Sometimes the artist can be a featured soloist in the music written by a film composer (such as Jerry Goldsmith's use of solo artists Pat Metheny in the score to *Under Fire* and Branford Marsalis in *Russia House*).

Another solution is to hire the pop/rock artist to write and perform songs for the Main Title, End Credits, or certain places in the body of the film, then hire a professional film composer to write the underscore (which you may or may not want to be in a similar style). These two options will give your film the prestige of having a famous pop/rock name attached to it without compromising the quality of the underscore.

Although most musicians are very versatile, there are limits. In short, it's not prudent to expect John Williams to produce the stylistic effect of Michael Jackson or Prince, nor is it prudent to hand over a 90-piece orchestra to a pop/rock recording artist.

3
COMMUNICATING WITH THE COMPOSER

You've hired a composer. You respect his music and trust that he's going to give his all for your film. Now comes the hard part: choosing words to communicate your creative vision—words that will be easily translated into music. This is the part of the filmmaking process in which most filmmakers feel a real loss of control. Every other element of the film has ways to preview the outcome fairly accurately, i.e., you can see real costumes, real makeup, and real sets/locations before shooting begins, but, unless your final score is completely electronic and being realized in the composer's home studio, there's usually no way to accurately hear the music score until you're on the recording stage with a live orchestra and can listen to playbacks with music, dialogue, and sound effects.

Many filmmakers have told me that communicating with the composer is one of the greatest challenges they face. It's difficult to find a common language (someone once said that trying to talk music is like trying to dance architecture). One of the most common errors filmmakers make is attempting to communicate with the composer using musical terms. This can lead to some monumental misunderstandings.*

The common language of the filmmaker and composer is one

---

* In his book *No Minor Chords,* Andre Previn describes an instance where the filmmaker's musical instructions, if taken literally, would have resulted in an entirely different score than was hoped for. During a chance encounter on the lot with a director whose film he was about to score, the director requested that the music have lots of French horns in it. Puzzled by such a specific request, Previn asked, "French horns?" "Yeah! You know! French horns!" the director replied, all the while pumping his arm furiously like a slide-trombone player. Had this conversation taken place on the telephone, the lack of visual clarification for the composer might have resulted in a nasty surprise on the scoring stage.

of emotion and drama. *The best method of communication is to tell the composer the emotion you want the audience to feel.*

When using words such as "powerful" or "intense," be sure to clearly define those terms. "Intense" can mean a vigorous, swirling effect in the orchestra, a powerful rock 'n' roll drum beat, or the slow, sad, painful intensity of Samuel Barber's *Adagio for Strings* (which was the score for Oliver Stone's *Platoon*). Playing different types of music during the film's rough cut (or even making a temp track *with the composer's help*) can be of great benefit in defining these words and your vision to the composer.

Although the filmmaker may have definite musical concepts in mind, it's still a good idea to listen to the composer's point of view, because the composer has a fresh perspective on the film, and his thoughts have not been colored by months of discussion with all the creative parties involved in the production. The composer may have a brilliant idea that nobody on the production team has thought of yet.

Making decisions by committee has become fairly common practice in the film industry and is a concern among composers (there's an old saw that goes, "Everybody on the picture knows his job and music, too"). *The main creative link should be between the composer and filmmaker.* For a large committee of people (film editor, music supervisor, music editor, three or four producers, plus a few studio executives) to attempt to find a single musical vision can be a circus. This sometimes leads to a score that's a generic hodge-podge of different music cues as the composer tries to please everyone.

One of the concerns most frequently expressed by composers today is the tendency for filmmakers to overcontrol all elements within a film score. This manifests itself from filmmakers wanting to preview every note of every cue in the score on synthesizer before going into the orchestral recording session to filmmakers making up their own musical themes on a piano at home and handing them to the composer. Analogously, a composer doesn't write out each wind instrument fingering, string bowing, or all the notes for a jazz/rock/country rhythm section; his job is to communicate an adequate amount of musical information, then set the atmosphere (musical and psychological) for a good performance.

The best performance comes from an artist using talent and experience to formulate the necessary professional judgement to carry out the task. Being overly controlling handcuffs the judgement of the artist and can result in a less-musical product.

In other words, give guidance, not instruction. The composer wants nothing more than to take your guidance and compose the most brilliant film score ever written; he really wants to please you. By being too "hands on" in the scoring process, the filmmaker can remove the composer's feeling of making a contribution, his creative passion. When the filmmaker "writes" the score himself, the composer is relegated to the status of musical lackey and his full creative potential is not utilized.

The following chapters should give you enough information to have the control you want, yet keep the composer/filmmaker creative relationship a positive, energized one.

4
THE ROUGH CUT

At the very latest, the composer should be hired during the early stages of the film's rough cut. The composer should screen first assemblies with the filmmaker and begin discussing the musical direction of the film. At this point, screenings and discussions are very beneficial. Now is the time to make artistic choices about whether the music will play with or against the action in a particular scene.

Spend time with the composer playing CDs of different types of music that you both feel may fit the film—a musical brainstorming. You may never find the exact sound that's right (which is the main reason for hiring a composer to write original music, remember), but you're exploring general musical concepts to communicate the heart and soul of your film to the audience.

I add a note of caution here: With easy access to hundreds of CDs and demo tapes, filmmakers tend to listen to these hoping to find their score already written somewhere. This is often a fruitless search. If the filmmaker does find something close, he may try to "shoehorn" it into the film. Worse yet, he may find something that he plays over and over, uses for the temp track, then falls in love with (sometimes rejecting the original music score written for the film, even if it's only slightly different). The primary job of the composer is to please the filmmaker. This practice often forces the composer to rewrite that beloved temp score, all the while dancing around the plagiarism issue.

After getting into the musical "ballpark," the composer can begin to sketch themes or general musical ideas and preview them for the filmmaker on piano or synthesizer. Remember, *this takes time*, so be sure that the postproduction schedule allows for it. Whenever the filmmaker wants to preview a cue or a theme, it requires time for a meeting, setting up the synths, programming the computer to play the synths, discussing the cue, perhaps making changes on the spot, etc. Unless the final score will be electronic, don't expect an accurate representation at this point, because there's no way a synthesizer can duplicate the intensity of a full orchestra; just use this to be sure that everybody is agreeing on the same musical concept.

If the decision is made to temp track the film, the composer can assist in that through the use of his record/CD library of film scores written by other composers, or, better yet, the tape library of original music he has written for previous films (using music that has his stylistic imprint may be a more accurate representation of the final score). The filmmaker and composer working together to create the temp track can be beneficial in communicating musical ideas; it makes for fewer surprises when it comes time to compose and record the actual score.

A warning about temp tracks: In some cases, the filmmaker hears the temp music version of the film so many times that he falls in love with it, and the real score subsequently ends up sounding alien and "wrong." This is especially true if the film has been temp tracked with a 90-piece orchestra, but the current working budget only allows for a 30-piece orchestra; the current, original score may be wonderfully written, but it won't have the same symphonic breadth as the temp and may be a letdown. Try not to listen to the temp track more than a few times; your musical palate should be clean so that the composer's original score is given an impartial hearing without being compared to the temp.

5
THE SPOTTING SESSION

In the spotting session, the filmmaker, composer, and music editor screen the locked picture and make final decisions about the beginning and ending of each music cue and what it's to say dramatically. Much of this will have been roughed in during the temp track or musical discussions during the rough cut. During the spotting session, the music editor makes spotting notes (see Example 1), which include a general description of the action and the footage numbers at the beginning and end of each cue. While making the spotting notes, the music editor assigns each cue a number (m11 or 1m1 means first reel, first music cue; m12 or 1m2 means first reel, second music cue; and so on). Afterward, the music editor retires to a video/computer setup and compiles and types up the timing notes, a detailed and accurate list of timings of each event within the music cue (see Example 2). The composer must have these exact timings so that he can weave the music into the scene, making the proper mathematical/musical calculations for hitting or missing certain events in the film. The music editor is able to begin this work only after a copy of the locked picture is delivered to him, and then it will take approximately two or three days for the timing notes to be completed and delivered to the composer so that he may begin writing.

Keep in mind that quite a bit of flexibility is allowed in the process of putting music to film. If, during the spotting session, a question arises about a particular place to start or stop a cue, the composer can write an alternate beginning or end so that there are options when the music is played back with dialogue and sound effects during the scoring session. This is something that typically may occur only a few times in a film; if it becomes com-

Production: **Heaven and Hell**

Episode: **PART III**

MUSIC SPOTTING NOTES

Monday, March 14, 1994

REEL 21   **(3 Starts)**

21m1   2:35.79   "MAIN TITLE #3"
  d1:00:10:02
  d1:02:45:25
  Background Instrumental

21m2   2:58.14   "Charlie & Scar Face Off"
  d1:02:45:25
  d1:05:44:00
  Background Instrumental

21m3   15.35   "Establish D.C."
  d1:07:35:05
  d1:07:50:15
  SPARSE PERCUSSION CUE

REEL 22   **(2 Starts)**

22m1   9.14   "Ashton/Chicago House"
  d2:04:51:04
  d2:05:00:10
  Background Instrumental

22m2   28.73   "To Tackett's Smithy"
  d2:07:35:24
  d2:08:04:17
  Background Instrumental

Example 1: Spotting notes as prepared by music editor Joanie Diener for the miniseries *North and South, Part 3.* [*Heaven and Hell* (David A. Bell), © 1994 WB Music Corp. All rights reserved. Used by permission.]

Production: **Heaven and Hell**   Episode: **PART III**

Cue: **30m2** "**Cooper and Gettys Die**"

Begins   at **d10:05:23:26** in Reel/Act 30

ABS. SMPTE #(df):	REL. TIME:		
			30m1 has just ended as Cooper shifted his aim toward Gettys - We CUT to CU Cooper as he shouts:"No!!"...
d10:05:23:26	0.00	CUT	MUSIC STARTS on MS Gettys - as Cooper finishes his yell (01.7 seconds after cut-off of 30m1)
d10:05:24:14	0.60		He FIRES
d10:05:25:05	1.30	CUT	MS Cooper as he is hit 1st time
d10:05:27:05	3.30	CUT	MS Gettys as he aims again
d10:05:28:02	4.20		FIRES
d10:05:28:12	4.54	CUT	CU Cooper as he's hit again - falling backwards
d10:05:29:09	5.44		And SPLASH!
d10:05:32:05	8.31		We HEAR a scared cry from Madeline
d10:05:32:26	9.01	CUT	MS George as he draws his gun
d10:05:34:04	10.28	CUT	MS Gettys as he rides forward
d10:05:35:09	11.44	CUT	MCU George aiming
d10:05:35:16	11.68		He FIRES
d10:05:37:02	13.21	CUT	MCU Gettys as he is hit - he examines the wound
d10:05:39:22	15.88	CUT	MCU George aiming
d10:05:40:09	16.45		FIRES again
d10:05:41:00	17.15	CUT	MS Gettys as he falls backward
d10:05:42:17	18.72	CUT	LONGER SHOT Gettys as he falls off horse
d10:05:42:25	18.98		Splash!
d10:05:44:20	20.82	CUT	MS a quivering Madeline against tree trunk as George reaches for her

Example 2: Music timing notes as prepared by music editor Joanie Diener for the miniseries *North and South, Part 3*. [*Heaven and Hell* (David A. Bell), © 1994 WB Music Corp. All rights reserved. Used by permission.]

mon practice, this indicates that the filmmaker and composer are not clear about their artistic vision. There is also a lot of flexibility and room for discussion in the recording session (this is covered later in the book).

Once the music editor has added up the total number of minutes of music in the film, the composer huddles with the producer, music supervisor, and music contractor to plan the number of hours of recording time that will be required to complete the score. The music contractor and composer juggle the size and type of orchestra to be used and create something that will fit the music budget. It's difficult to generalize, but if using any kind of acoustic instrumental ensemble in a recording-studio setting, a good rule of thumb is to figure on recording three minutes of music per hour (usually a bit more per hour for television and low-budget theatrical films, a bit less per hour for high-budget theatrical films). This can be increased to four or five minutes per hour if the music is easy to perform and there is little or no discussion between filmmaker and composer, few playbacks, few changes, etc. More about this in Chapter 15 regarding budgets.

During the first week after the spotting session, the composer must organize a myriad of administrative details, such as reserving the recording studio, booking the scoring mixer (sometimes a bit of juggling is necessary for the composer to book his favorite recording stage on the same days that his favorite scoring mixer is available), drawing up the list of musicians for the music contractor to call, arranging payroll details, organizing orchestrators, copyists, etc. Much of this is taken care of by the music supervisor/music department at major studios, but if working for an independent production company without a fully involved music supervisor (especially on a package deal), a lot of the composer's composing time and energy is diverted by these administrative details. This has been a major change in the film composer's life— in the "good old days," a composer only had to concern himself with meetings with the filmmaker, writing the score, and conducting the recording sessions.

This is also the time when the music contractor is busiest. Under the best of circumstances, it takes the music contractor and his telephone booking service several days to call even a small orchestra. The first round of phone calls is sent out to the composer's preferred musicians, and it takes a couple days for those people to return with a "yes" or "no" answer. The second call then goes out to find alternates for those who weren't available. The same sifting process continues for several days until the orchestra list is complete. Even after the orchestra is set, minor shufflings continue right up to the day of scoring—musicians have schedule changes, or the composer adds or subtracts a few players, or the entire schedule of scoring sessions is changed by the production company for some reason. The best musicians and recording studios in Los Angeles are usually booked *at least* two or three weeks in advance, so the earlier the session can be scheduled and the musicians called, the better.

(Budget note: If the musicians are canceled within ninety-six hours of the beginning of the recording session, they receive full salary for that day.)

6
THE COMPOSING PROCESS

With the timing notes in hand, the composer can begin to write the score, weaving the music into the scene so that it enhances, not fights, the action, dialogue, and sound effects. This is a difficult component of the craft to learn and is where experience really counts. The experienced film composer has spent thousands of hours painstakingly writing notes and then has studied how they fit with the other elements of the dubbed films, each time learning more about his art.

This can be a difficult time for the filmmaker because, with the exception of occasional meetings with the composer, he must sit back and wait a few weeks while the music is being written. The filmmaker has had a great deal of hands-on control during the making of the film, but now he must be patient and let the composer work his magic.

On the average, a composer can write approximately two or three minutes of music per day after the main themes have been approved by the filmmaker (this should have been done during the rough cut). This daily output is a very general number and depends on the complexity of the music, the size of the ensemble, the amount of time spent in meetings and discussions with the filmmaker, etc. As he's writing, the composer can preview some of the cues for the filmmaker on piano or home synthesizer and refine them. Some composers refer to this synthesizer preview as making a musical "Polaroid" and, unless the final score will be synthesized, should be used only to ensure that the composer and filmmaker agree on the general musical concept. If the final score is completely synthesized and being produced in the composer's home studio, it's possible to meet with the composer every few days and hear the actual cues that have been completed to that date. If the music is acoustic/orchestral, it's usually best to wait until the actual recording session to begin making detailed refinements—there's simply no way a synthesizer or piano can duplicate the symphonic breadth of an orchestra. As long as the music is "in the ballpark," changes can easily be made on the recording stage if the composer is experienced in the art of film scoring.

The directorial equivalent of judging a synthesizer mock-up of an orchestral score would be for the studio financing the picture to ask the filmmaker to preview all scenes using a home camcorder and a high-school drama club. The chill you felt up your spine as you read that last sentence is how most composers feel when asked to preview orchestral scores on synthesizer. The only way to make a clear judgement about a the score is to have the composer's true musical vision presented in the recording session with the full orchestra and the cues played back locked to picture with a rough mix of dialogue, music, and sound effects. The experienced film composer can make alterations on the scoring stage, revising the music until you're completely satisfied (subject to budget restrictions, of course).

During those weeks that the composer is writing the music, it may be tempting to make a few editorial nips and tucks, but try to avoid this. If done in the middle of a music cue, it throws off the composer's timings and can wreak havoc in the score—in fact, from the composer's point of view, the cutting of a few frames can sometimes be worse than cutting several seconds. If the composer has completed a cue and the film is changed, it usually has repercussions all the way down the line: The music editor must retime that scene and type up new timing notes, the composer must alter or rewrite the cue, the cue must be reorchestrated, the copyists have to recopy, etc. If this is done occasionally, it's tolerable (and expected), but a constant fiddling with the film after it's locked will make for an unhappy music team, and the final product may suffer a bit. If major editing continues past the spotting session, give the composer extra days or weeks to rewrite the cues he's completed or, if that's not possible, increase the budget for the employment of additional orchestrators and/or co-writers. Every composer I know wants to give his blood, sweat, and tears to a score; the filmmaker can help foster this by creating a reasonable environment in which the composer may work.

As the composer completes the musical sketches of a few cues (Example 3), he hands them over to the orchestrator, who transcribes that material into the full orchestral score (Example 4). As the orchestrator completes that batch of fully orchestrated cues, they are delivered to the music librarian and copyists, who hand-copy* each individual instrumental part (Example 5), number them, record the cue numbers, timings, titles, and instrumentation onto a breakdown sheet (Example 6), place each part into a book for each specific instrument, then bring it all to the recording session and place each book on the appropriate music stand. The music librarian and orchestrator must be at the recording session in case any changes/rewrites take place and need to be hand-copied into each instrumental part. To save money, it's most economical to do this when the orchestra is on a break.

The composer communicates to the music editor information such as event timings, tempo rates, placement of visual streamers, etc. on sketches, scores, and/or through the use of computer MIDI files. The music editor then begins to prepare the playback video, recording tape and session computer, generating streamers, lining up the beginnings and endings of music cues and clix, etc. The composer/conductor uses all of these tools to make the music synch with the film. See Chapter 10 on the music editor's job for more detailed treatment of this.

---

* Although instrumental parts are increasingly being computer generated, a lot of human input and correcting is needed because musical language is complex and the computer rarely gets it right.

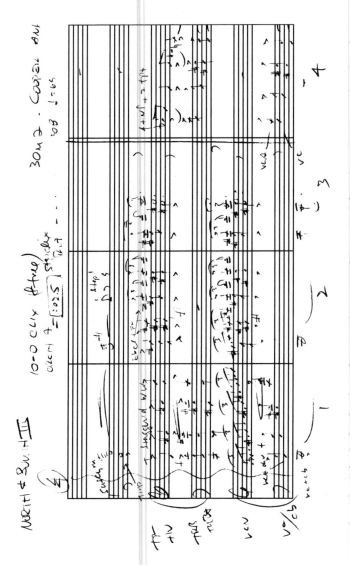

Example 3: Sketch for the first four bars of cue 3m2 ("Cooper and Gettys Die") from the miniseries *North and South, Part 3*. Composed by David Bell. The expanded and fully orchestrated version of this is shown in Example 4. [*Heaven and Hell* (David A. Bell), © 1994 WB Music Corp. All rights reserved. Used by permission.]

Example 4: Orchestral score of the first four bars of cue 30m2 from the miniseries *North and South, Part 3*. Composed and orchestrated by David Bell. [*Heaven and Hell* (David A. Bell), © 1994 WB Music Corp. All rights reserved. Used by permission.]

Violin

Heaven & Hell

30m2

Example 5: First page of the violin part for cue 30m2 from the miniseries *North and South, Part 3*. [*Heaven and Hell* (David A. Bell), © 1994 WB Music Corp. All rights reserved. Used by permission.]

A ORCHESTRA

COMPOSER: DAVID BELL
ORCH.: DAVID BELL

STUDIO: CAPITOL A
DATE: SCHEDULED JAN 11-12, 1994
TIME: @ AM DOUBLES

PRODUCTION: NORTH & SOUTH BOOK III
TITLE: HEAVEN & HELL

REEL	PART	TITLE	DUBS	TIME	NO. OF BARS	3	3	2	OB	CL	BSN	HORN	f+t+s	tba	PERCUSSION				HARP	VIOLIN	VIOLA	CELLO	BASS
1	1	MAIN TITLE #1	D. BELL	2:35	65	Fl	Fl (Picc.)	Fl	OB	Bass Cl. Cl.	Contra BSN	4	2	2/1	Sus. Cym.	Concert Cym. Field Dm(w/Sn)	Bass Dm. Field Dm.(no snare)	Timp.	—	16	8	6	4
1		BUMPER #1	D. Mello	:06	2	Fl	Fl	Fl	OB	B.cl Bcl	B.cl. BSN	4	2	2/1	Sus. Cym.	Concert C.ym.	Timp.	—	16	8	6	4
1		BUMPER #2	D. BELL	:06	2	Fl	Fl	Fl	OB	Cl Bcl Cl BU	Bn	4	2	2/1	—	—	—	—	16	8	6	4
1	2	CARRIAGE IN FOG	D. BELL	2:00	24	Fl	Fl	Fl	E.H.	Cl Bcl.Cl BN	Bn	4	1	2/1	VIBES (w/ bows)	—	B.D.	Timp.	—	16	8	6	4
1	3	BENT STASS DEEV	D. BELL	2:00	35	Fl	Fl	Fl	E.H. OB	Cl Perc Cl BN	Bn	4	2	2/1	Vibes(w/bows) Sus Cym.	Field Dm. (w/ snare)	Field Dm. Cym. Cym-Snare Bass Dm.	Timp.	—	16	8	6	4
1	4	ASHTON PUSHES BENT	D. BELL	1:40	26	Fl	Picc	Fl	OB E.H.	Cl BN	CBN	4	2	2/1	Vibes(w/bows) Sus Cym.	Suspo	B.D.	Timp.	—	16	8	6	4
4	2	GEORGE RIDES TO MONT ROYAL	D. BELL	2:25	47	Fl	Fl	Fl	OB	Cl BN	BN	4	1	2/1	Sus Cym	Field Dm.	Field Dm Timp	Timp.	—	16	8	6	4
4	3	BENT IN HOUSE	D. BELL	1:35	24	Fl	—	Fl	EH	Cl Cl BN	BN	4	2	2/1	—	—	—	Timp.	—	16	8	6	4
4	1	GED, MAD MAD SHAKE IN 15	D. BELL	1:05	20	Fl	Picc	Fl	EH OB	Cl B.cl. Bcl.	Bn	4	2	2/1	Sus. Cym.	—	B.D.	Timp.	—	16	8	6	4
10	3	END CREDITS	D. BELL	1:00	42/25	Fl	Fl	Fl	OB	Cl BN	Bcal. CBN	4	2	2/1	Congas	As Are Field Dm. Part.	Part / Timp.	Timp.	—	16	8	6	4
8	3	MORGANS SONGS LONGFORM	D. BELL	2:10	41	Fl	Fl	Fl	OB	Cl Bcl.Cl BN	Bn	4	2	2/1	Indian Tom	Field Dm Tom Field Dm.	Field Dm Timp Bass Dm (w/ snare) Cym	Timp.	—	16	8	6	4
8	4	SLOE WINCHES THRU LEBLE VILLAGE	D. BELL	:15	8	—	—	—	—	— C. Bn	—	4	—	—	Indian Tom	Suspo	B.D.	Timp.	—	16	8	6	4

Example 6: Orchestra breakdown sheet showing instrumentation, number of performers needed, and durations of music cues. This information is used to efficiently schedule the sequence in which the cues are recorded. [*Heaven and Hell* (David A. Bell), © 1994 WB Music Corp. All rights reserved. Used by permission.]

7
THE RECORDING SESSION

This is the place where the filmmaker has more control and flexibility than most people are aware of. Once a music cue has been recorded, play it back with dialogue and sound effects and discuss it. Most likely, the filmmaker will be initially thrilled (after waiting for so long, *anything* played by a large orchestra is going to sound impressive!). However, as the recording session progresses, there will probably be more calls for the composer to make minor adjustments in the score (he may even volunteer a few himself). This is a fairly uncomplicated process (especially with an experienced film composer), and requests by the filmmaker for the music to be slower, faster, thinner, darker, lighter, etc., are easily accommodated. Occasionally, the need will arise to make major alterations to a cue, which can be done on the lunch break or over night (assuming that more than one day of scoring was scheduled).

SCORING SESSION BASICS

This section describes the traditional method of scoring with an acoustic ensemble on a commercial recording stage. This is the foundation for much of what happens during the recording of a synthesized score produced in a home studio (which is described at the end of this chapter).

The typical television movie or low-budget film contains thirty to forty minutes of music and will require one to two days to record; the average high-budget film requires three to five days.* The army of musicians, a music librarian, a contractor, a scoring

* Scoring a motion picture usually takes longer because virtually every cue is played back and discussed, optional versions of cues written and recorded, etc.

The author conducting a recording session and listening to playback. [Photographs by Lester Cohen.]

TIME	CUE #	NAME	LENGTH	TOTAL
10:00-10:50 a.m.	10m3	End Credits	1:00	
	?	2 Bumpers @ :06 each	0:12	
	1m1	Main Title #1 (recap)	2:35	
	11m1	Main Title #2 (reuse for #3)	2:45	
				6:30
11:00-11:50 a.m.	1m2	Carriage in Fog	2:00	
	1m3	Bent Stabs Orry	2:00	
	1m4	Ashton Pushes Bent	1:40	
				5:40
12:00-12:50 p.m.	4m2	George Rides to Mont Royal	2:25	
	4m3	Bent in Alms House	1:35	
	5m1	Geo. and Mad. Shake on it	1:05	
				5:05
1:00-2:00 p.m.		LUNCH		
2:00-2:50 p.m.	6m3	Venable's Boys Beat Charlie	1:06	
	7m1	Ben Ellis/Travois	0:40	
	7m2	Handshake/Sunset	0:20	
	7m4	New Sawmill	1:18	
	8m3	Yanking Scar's Loincloth	2:10	
				5:30
3:00-3:50 p.m.	8m4	Scar Watches Them Leave Village	0:25	
	9m2	The Klan Rides	0:30	
	9m3	Klan Arrives at Mont Royal	1:05	
	9m4	Klan Burns the School	2:04	
	10m1	Bent Under the Stairs	0:40	
				4:45
4:00-4:50 p.m.	10m2	Bent Kills Constance	2:20	
				2:20
				29:50
5:00-5:30 p.m. O.T.	17m1	Isaac's Convention Spch (Orch "C")	2:50	
5:30- 2 GUITARS	5m5	Lazy Cantina Source	1:20	
	6m4	Party Cantina Source	1:00	

"N S III" Orch "A"   (TUESDAY)

Scoring schedule for a recording session. 10:00 A.M. to 4:50 P.M. utilizes full orchestra (Orchestra A). In the overtime period beginning at 5:00 P.M., the orchestra is reduced to strings only (Orchestra C) and finally to just two guitars at 5:30.

mixer, etc., assembles on the appointed day with usually a 9:00 or 10:00 A.M. start time or "downbeat." The cues probably will not be recorded in the order in which they appear in the film: Over the course of these two to five days, the composer and music contractor will have planned the recording sessions so that the cues with the largest orchestra are recorded first, then musicians are released as the orchestral requirements diminish in size. The purpose of this is to save money (for instance, the intimate romantic cues probably will not need six percussionists, ten brass, and so on).

The musicians are hired in three-hour blocks of time with a ten-minute break each hour. Three to five minutes of finished music are scored per hour. Usually, a television episode with less than fifteen minutes of music will be scored in one three-hour session (referred to as a "single" session) with an hour of overtime if required. A production containing twenty to thirty minutes of underscore will typically require two three-hour blocks of time (a "double" session) with an hour of prorated overtime if necessary.

It will take the scoring mixer twenty to thirty minutes to get the microphones balanced into the proper mix; in other words, the first hour will go slowly, but the speed will pick up almost exponentially as the musicians and scoring mixer get the musical style of this particular score under their fingers. I never cease to be amazed at what an incredibly well-oiled machine the Hollywood scoring session is. The musicians have never seen the music until they sit down that day; their sightreading abilities are nothing less than astonishing. Add to that the work done by everyone else on the recording stage and the event is a thing of wonder.

The composer uses two basic methods to make sure that the performance of the orchestra matches the film. The first is by conducting "free time" while watching the podium clock (a large clock with a sweep-second hand); this method gives the music a natural, emotional ebb and flow. There may be important points within the cue where the music and action coordinate exactly, and the composer will have instructed the music editor to draw a streamer leading to that point. As the composer/conductor approaches the streamer, he is able to gauge by the clock if he is conducting in approximately the right time so that when the streamer works its way across the screen (the film is projected on a large wall-screen opposite the conductor or a television monitor for video), he can give the exact conducting motion necessary at the precise time to synch the music with the dramatic event. The second, and most precise, way to coordinate the musicians' performance with the film is to use clicks (or clix): an audible clicking noise generated by a digital metronome or computer that the musicians hear in their headphones. This sounds a bit robotic for slow, emotional cues, but is very handy for anything that has a steady tempo (i.e., chase cues).

MAKING CHANGES ON THE RECORDING STAGE

Now is the best time for the filmmaker to begin shaping the score to his liking. The film, some of the sound effects, and most of the dialogue are available at the recording session to include with the playback of the music cues so that the true impact of the music as it relates to these other elements can be properly measured and discussed. If the communication between filmmaker and composer took place early enough and often enough to agree on the general style of the music, no major rewrites should be needed: It's all a matter of fine-tuning at this point. Once again, this is where the experience of the composer who specializes in film scoring is extremely valuable: Being able to make changes on the recording stage quickly and efficiently (remember, the orchestra is "on the clock") is a craft that requires a lot of practice.

The recording session is one of the most crucial collaborative times between the composer and filmmaker; it's important that the communication be clear and concise so that the music serves the filmmaker's vision and time is not wasted while the orchestra is on the time clock. It's probably a good idea for the composer and filmmaker to spend some time together before the recording session discussing the most effective ways of expressing musical/dramatic ideas to each other.

Generally, it's best to "cut to the chase" during these recording-session discussions—especially when working under budget and time constraints. Going into lengthy discussions about the motives of each character in the scene is not very helpful or efficient; that should have been done during the initial discussions in prior weeks. For instance, use general terms during playback to help the composer shape the music at specific points: "It should be darker, more ominous," "It should be less busy, more sparse," "Brighter, crisper," "Point out the murder clue lying on the table more," "Don't point out the murder clue on the table," or "At the section when the girl says the climactic line, the music is getting in the way." Let the composer figure out the best way to make the necessary changes, then dictate them to the musicians to be penciled into their parts.

Again, be cautious about getting too specific with musical terminology. Instead of saying, "Get that saxophone out of there, it's too busy," simply express your feelings that the saxophone is fighting the scene somehow and needs to be changed. The composer may have the saxophonist play softer, or play in a lower octave, or delete some notes, or change to a different saxophone, or have the part played on another instrument, or even drop the part entirely. Remember that the composer chose to put that saxophone in that particular place with those particular notes for what he regarded as a crucial dramatic reason. There are many, many options to solve any problems the filmmaker may have with the score, and it's best to let the composer explore these options so that he can satisfy the filmmaker, yet still have a score that makes musical sense.

Try this: Play back the cue with dialogue and sound effects as the composer stands with you in the booth, score in hand. Do a running commentary such as, "This first section is good . . . this part here is too busy during the dialogue (composer makes note of that on score page) . . . I like this next section OK . . . but this last part isn't dark enough, it needs to be more threatening . . ." Keep your comments as short as possible, then elaborate when the playback is finished.

A big no-no is for the filmmaker to play the role of music arranger. If a cue needs to be changed, communicate the mood or flavor you want the music to have. Do not begin to arrange the music yourself by asking for a second version of the cue to be recorded with the sax playing the solo, a third version with the trumpet playing the solo, a fourth version with the sax playing the first part of the solo and the trumpet playing the second part, and so on, until the musicians want to mutiny. If the content of the film and the communication with the composer reflect a focused creative vision on the part of the filmmaker, there should be no need for this kind of thing to happen. I cannot stress enough how destructive this is to the music and, ultimately, the film; part of the job of the composer/conductor is to create a session atmosphere that will get the most inspired performances from the musicians. The filmmaker should do everything possible to foster that.

Most composers conduct their own scores, so they are assisted by a music sound consultant (usually the orchestrator), who sits in the mixing booth next to the scoring mixer and reads from a copy of the full score, calling out cues for solos, helping with the balance, etc. Communicate with this person and the scoring mixer occasionally as they may be able to clarify things for you, or act as an immediate conduit of information between you and the composer. For instance, if you find a particular musical event bothersome as a music cue is being rehearsed to picture ("what's that cymbal crash doing on that dialogue line?"), communicate it immediately to the music sound consultant. He can then make a note on the score and, when the rehearsal is finished, draw the composer's attention to it by speaking through the intercom and giving the composer an exact location by referring to a measure number. Or the music consultant can tell you that the cymbal crash is not supposed to be there, that the percussionist miscounted and played in the wrong place. The music consultant and scoring mixer can be a big help in the communication process as long as all parties are careful not to undermine the relationship between the composer and filmmaker.

An experienced composer and music contractor will know how to make the filmmaker/composer creative discussions most efficient. For instance, for every hour of stage time, the musicians work fifty minutes with a ten-minute break. There is some flexibility as to when these breaks occur, so if the filmmaker is not at all happy with a cue that has just been recorded and wants to engage in a lengthy discussion, it might be a good idea to give the musicians a ten-minute break while the cue is played back with film, dialogue, and sound effects. This can save a lot of money in overtime costs over the course of a two- or three-day scoring session. The composer and contractor should be experienced enough to gauge this sort of thing.

If you are unhappy with a particular cue and the composer

just isn't able to understand the direction you want the music to take, relate your ideas to a previous cue in the score, such as, "Remember the cue in reel three when the girl is cowering in the corner in fear? That's the kind of feel I want in this scene, too." The composer can either quickly adapt that same cue to fit the scene you're discussing or compose a variation of it on a lunch break or over night. The point is, once you get into the recording session and hear the music in its full glory, a better basis for discussion is established (especially if you have a reasonable budget that allows time for discussion).

If there are cues where you've asked the composer to make changes, keep his original version handy at the dub just in case it seems to work well when played with final sound effects and dialogue tracks. You may dislike a cue in the recording session, which, after lunch or on replay the next day, may work perfectly now that it's better understood within the context of the score as a whole.

This is also true if there are questions about the mix. You may find that the scoring mixer's original mix works better in the final dub. Part of his job is to know what the music will sound like after being subjected to several transfers and the final dub (plus satellite transmissions and television broadcast in some cases). I once worked on a project, where, over the strong objections of the scoring mixer and myself, the filmmaker insisted on raising the volume of the electric bass part. When the music was broadcast over the television airwaves, it sounded like an electric bass solo; the rest of the band was lost and it sounded ridiculous. The point is, give the composer and scoring mixer the benefit of the doubt; they usually know their business.

It's crucial for the filmmaker to attend all music scoring sessions, because if the necessary changes aren't made there, it inevitably leads to attempting musical changes in the dub, which is a recipe for disaster.

HOME-STUDIO SCORING

A home-studio synthesized score will most likely be constructed one cue at a time—in its complete and final form—so the filmmaker should make numerous trips to the composer's studio to hear the progress of the score. In this way, any of the filmmaker's changes that have an impact on cues farther into the score can be addressed immediately. If acoustic instruments are to be added later ("sweetening"), they can be temporarily represented by synthesizer stand-in tracks until the final session, when the sweetening is done. This can mean the addition of only one or two acoustic instruments (or voices) in a recording session at the composer's studio or the addition of a whole symphony orchestra at a large commercial recording studio. Once in the sweetening session with the acoustic ensemble, changes in mix or orchestration are easy to make, but changes in tempo requested by the filmmaker at this stage are very difficult—the master tape with the synthesized musical foundation must be returned to the composer's studio and rerecorded at a different tempo, then the acoustic ensemble (and commercial recording studio) must be rehired for another session. However, this rarely happens because the synthesizer "Polaroids" done at the composer's studio are usually accurate enough to gauge proper tempo.

8
COMPOSERS, ORCHESTRATORS, ARRANGERS, GHOSTWRITERS, HUMMERS, AND PLAGIARISTS

How much of the score does a composer actually write? Most composers need some help from time to time (especially when trying to meet a tight deadline), but there are rules (some defined by the American Federation of Musicians) of collegial, professional guidelines/ethics that help to define the terms heading this chapter.

As a filmmaker, you may not think that it's important whether your score is written by one composer or a team of ghostwriters. It *is* important because a composer who writes (and thereby is familiar with) his own music will save time and money on the recording stage by being able to make quick changes, and the score will have a distinctive, powerful style rather than the generic Hollywood sound of the ghostwritten score.

Composing is a hard-won art (studies have shown that writing for a symphony orchestra is one of the most complex human brain activities), and many film composers committed to the integrity of the art are concerned with the increase in ghostwriting in today's film industry. Some of the biggest films in Hollywood are scored by folks who call themselves "composers," yet who hardly know up from down, musically speaking. This is largely due to hiring a younger, "hip" generation of music writers who don't know their craft as well as they should and who employ orchestrators, ghostwriters, and electronic technicians to do the work for them; they are businesspeople first and composers second. Few of today's scores are in the same league as those classics written by Bernard Herrmann (*Psycho, Vertigo*), Jerry Goldsmith (*Patton,*

Planet of the Apes), Elmer Bernstein (*The Magnificent Seven, To Kill a Mockingbird*), John Addison (*Sleuth, Tom Jones*), David Raksin (*Laura, The Bad and the Beautiful*), Henry Mancini (*Breakfast at Tiffany's, The Pink Panther*), Alex North (*A Streetcar Named Desire, Spartacus*), Laurence Rosenthal (*The Miracle Worker, Becket*), John Williams (*Star Wars* trilogy, *The Witches of Eastwick*), and more recently Bruce Broughton (*Silverado, Young Sherlock Holmes*). These gentlemen are true composers whose complete grasp of melody, harmony, counterpoint, and orchestration allows them to write scores rich in texture and dramatic depth.

The following are general categories describing those working in film music today.

COMPOSERS

A composer is one who writes out all of the notes of a score and has complete knowledge and control of all the elements, such as note choices, tempo, orchestration, etc. In the classical sense, composers such as Mozart, Beethoven, Ravel, Copland, and Stravinsky would never have conceived of separating the disciplines of composing and orchestrating, for true composition is the integration of the two. However, with the time constraints of Hollywood, this is rarely possible, so the two disciplines have become partitioned to various degrees; often it simply isn't humanly possible to write out the full music score in the time allowed. Even today's best Hollywood film composers must write out a detailed sketch (a short-hand version of the final orchestral score) and have that expanded to the full score by an orchestrator.

The term "composer" has become blurred in recent years with the advent of the synthesizer—now a person with little or no musical training can create a musical score with a little knowledge of music electronics. This is *not* to say that anyone who uses a synthesizer is untrained. Quite the contrary: All composers in Hollywood use synthesizers in one capacity or another. However, it is easier now for the untrained composer to hide deficiencies with push-button technology. Too many filmmakers have been dazzled by the technology and hired composers without real compositional craft, which has resulted in many music scores in recent years being merely adequate in quality.

The best-composed music is that which is originally conceived for specific colors or instrumentation. Take, for instance, the score John Williams wrote for *The Witches of Eastwick.* One of the main characteristics of the music is a triple-time figure designed for a solo violin or section of violins that is rooted in the "devilish" sounds of some 18th and 19th century Italian music (i.e., the Tarantella). This could only have been written by a composer with a thorough understanding of the orchestra and the history of classical music. Furthermore, this style of music must be played by a violin (or violins) to have the proper effect; it wouldn't transfer well to synthesizer. The melodies were conceived with the entire musical package in mind, not just a patching together of various musical elements. Although John Williams used the services of a great orchestrator, Herb Spencer, Mr. Williams' sketches have always been thorough, and he has complete creative control and understanding of every note that goes on the final score page.

The same would be true for a filmmaker looking for a more contemporary, jazz/pop/rock music score; it would be logical to search for a composer who has both a classical and jazz/pop/rock background such as Tom Newman, James Newton Howard, or Mark Isham. These are people who have a full understanding of all the components of a rhythm "groove" plus a thorough, "schooled" knowledge of acoustic/orchestral instruments that allows for thoughtful, intelligent stretching of musical boundaries. Note especially Mark Isham's score to *Never Cry Wolf;* it was fully conceived and performed for a specific combination of synthesizers and acoustic instruments. The acoustic instrumental parts would sound awkward if played on a synthesizer, and the synthesized parts would sound awkward if performed on acoustic instruments. This is true, complete composing.

ORCHESTRATORS

"Orchestration," as defined by the *Harvard Dictionary of Music,* is "the art of employing, in an instrumental composition, the various instruments in accordance with (a) their individual properties and (b) the composer's concept of the sonorous effect of his work. It involves a detailed knowledge of the playing mechanism of each instrument, its range, tone quality, loudness, limitations, etc." This last sentence is a key one, for the best, most distinctive Hollywood scores come from composers who have a complete knowledge of the orchestra or other instrumental/electronic ensembles with which they're working.

Ideally, a composer begins by conceptualizing all the musical elements necessary for the score and then discusses these concepts with the orchestrator. It's best when melodies and instrumentation are invented together, much like the drawstrings on a bag: All sides come together at the same time to create a final closure. If the composer has decided to use an oboe solo as a main thematic element, the melody needs to be designed to match the characteristics of that instrument or of related instruments that will also play the theme.

Take, for example, the brilliant opening music for the film *The Mission*, composed by Ennio Morricone. The various musical elements represent specific dramatic concepts and are layered on top of one another; English horn solo (similar to an oboe, but deeper and richer in color), strings, percussion, vocal chorus. All the parts were conceived and beautifully written for those specific instruments; if those musical lines would have been transferred to any other instrument, the music would have been much less effective. This score couldn't have been realized without a thorough understanding of the register, texture, timbre (color), dynamic properties, etc., of the instruments involved.

STANDARD WORKING PROCESS

As the process unfolds in the typical Hollywood manner, the composer begins sketching the music on a 6- to 12-stave page (Example 3, page 32), then hands that off to the orchestrator to expand that short-hand information to the full-size 20- to 30-stave score page (Example 4, page 33) so that the music copyists can extract the individual instrumental parts (Example 5, page 34). Exceptions to this are most television productions or low-budget films, for which the composer will usually orchestrate his own work. As mentioned above, the sketch is a short-hand version of the score and, when done by the best composers, clearly shows the complete musical vision of the composer with dynamics, voicings, etc.; the music copyists could almost extract the instrumental parts from the sketch.

Although not an exact analogy, the literary equivalent would be the author who writes in long-hand, then hands off those pages to an editor and typesetter to be checked, spaced, and set neatly. As the music score progresses, the sketches can become less and less detailed as the orchestrator becomes more familiar with the style. When I began my career, I orchestrated for John Addison and Laurence Rosenthal on occasion, and both of these gentlemen's sketches had almost every note written out on a condensed 6- to 8-line staff; orchestrating in instances such as these requires very little creativity—it's a matter of sorting out (putting all the notes for an orchestra on six to eight lines can be cramped and difficult to read) and expanding the sketch to the full orchestral score page, thereby making it neat enough for the copyists to do their work.

A step down the creative ladder from the above is the composer who knows his craft, but who, for reasons of time restraints (or laziness), doesn't write out too many notes. His sketches are very sketchy, and he relies on an orchestrator to do most of the actual composing.

FILM MUSIC MOGULS

In recent years there has been an increase in the number of what I call "film music moguls." These are composers or music producers who employ a staff or "stable" of (usually) young composers who do the actual writing and recording of the scores. These film music factories can churn out hundreds of hours of product per year. Even though the film music mogul may have little or no involvement with the actual composing, he or she often takes a portion—or, in the worst cases, all—of the composing royalties.

ARRANGERS

"Arranging" usually involves more note choices than orchestration; it falls in the area between composing and orchestrating and involves (1) working with previously existing melody written by the composer or (2) making a new arrangement of another piece of music in the standard literature.

For instance, in the first case, the orchestral composer may only be able to write 50% to 75% of a big-band jazz music cue and will need the services of an arranger, whose specialty is fine-tuning the instrumental voicings; i.e., to structure the writing for the saxes, trumpets, and trombones to be sure that the style is specific to the needs of the film (so that the music sounds like Glenn Miller rather than Count Basie, for example).

In the second case, the filmmaker may want a popular rock 'n' roll tune to be arranged for string quartet or a Mozart string quartet piece to be arranged for rock 'n' roll band.

GHOSTWRITERS

Regrettably, more and more "composers" writing for the film industry are businessmen first and composers second. Their main talent is in getting the job; they talk a good line and "give good interview." Their compositional craft is minimal to completely nonexistent, so they hire orchestrators/arrangers or less-established composers to do most (if not all) of the work for them by ghostwriting the score. This reaches a point where the "orchestrator" is making a lot of creative decisions and should be compensated more than the base scale wage (i.e., shared royalties, screen credit, overscale wages). Ghostwriting is becoming much too common in Hollywood, especially in the younger generation of "composers"; it's usually due to laziness, lack of musical training, greed, or looming deadlines.

This costs the studio/production company much more money than is necessary, because, one way or another, they're paying for that extra help of the ghostwriter when the "composer" is unable to perform his legitimate function.

HUMMERS

Those who *need* to hire ghostwriters due to their lack of composing skills are called "hummers."

A "hummer" has virtually no musical training, but merely hums (or plays one-finger piano) a melody that is then used by the real composer(s)/ghostwriter(s) to create the score. This, too, usually results in a generic, uninteresting musical score and is usually more expensive. This is somewhat palatable if the hummer calls himself a "music producer" or "tunester" and shares the royalties with those who created the music. But he isn't a composer.

PLAGIARISTS

Film composers are rarely asked to write anything truly original. One reason for this is because, by nature of the beast, most film music must have a prior aural association for the audience. The victorious scene needs victorious music, the romantic scene needs romantic music, and so forth.

Another reason is the increased use of temp tracking. Although temp tracks have been used for decades for studio and test screenings, only in recent years has the intent of the temp track been to guide the composer toward a musical style and concept. While some filmmakers use a temp track to communicate a "flavor" of their wishes for the final score, others are very specific and want the final score to be very, very close to the temp track. This often results in a score that is just outside the boundaries of a copyright infringement. This not only creates a moral dilemma for most composers ("If I want to please the filmmaker so he'll keep my score intact and perhaps hire me again in the future, I'd better not deviate from the temp track"), but is artistically constraining—most composers would prefer to be pointed in a general musical direction, then given creative leeway to write something original to benefit the film.

Composing music that "sounds like" Copland is much different than composing music that "is" Copland almost note for note; yet, time and again, some composers consciously cross that line of distinction.

Sometimes, plagiarism is unintentional; after all, there are only twelve notes in the octave, and some might say that most of the mathematical possibilities of different ordering of those notes were used up long ago . . .

* * *

The point is, it's best to work with a composer who has complete craft. It's less costly and much better creatively. A well-trained and experienced film composer will be able to communicate with the filmmaker directly and compose a score with a strong, distinctive musical vision that hasn't been filtered through ghostwriters.

9
THE MUSIC SUPERVISOR

There are basically two categories of music supervisors: the independent music supervisor and the studio music director.* Their level of involvement differs from project to project, and they may do all or only a selected few of the duties listed below (some projects don't even require the services of a music supervisor). Working on a film that has a qualified music supervisor on board makes life easier for everyone, because (1) logistical details and creative communication between composer and filmmaker are greatly facilitated, and (2) creative song selection and negotiating skills with publishers and record companies can result in a very strong (and financially lucrative) soundtrack.

The music supervisor's duties:

- After reading the script and having creative discussions with the filmmaker, he helps create the music budget based on estimated requirements of song purchases and size of underscore ensemble. In many cases, the music budget is in place before a music supervisor is attached to the project and, if the numbers are unrealistic, he may have to lobby hard for increased funding to meet the needs of the script and the filmmaker's musical vision.

- If applicable, he organizes prerecords prior to shooting. This can mean helping to select preexisting songs or

---

* Because of corporate structure, the studio music director is usually given an official title such as Director of Television Music or Senior Vice President of Music. To simplify matters, most composers refer to them as "the head of film (or television) music at such-and-such studio."

helping to choose composer/songwriters/artists to write original material. The music supervisor will oversee the music editor and the playback equipment, help coordinate any musicians or dancers who will appear on set, and ensure that actors/sideline musicians who are on set are in synch with the playback.

• He helps the filmmaker sift through the many composer submissions from agents, trying to match a composer's style/ability, fee range, and personality to the picture and the filmmaker. Even if the filmmaker favors a composer with whom he's worked before, it's the music supervisor's job to play devil's advocate and ensure that that composer is indeed the best person for the job. A note for consideration: some music supervisors and studios have strong relationships with certain composers or agents and will push for these choices—it's a safe, reliable, no-surprises situation as far as they're concerned. However, by doing this, the filmmaker may not be seeing/hearing the full range of choices available. This is not so much a criticism as it is a fact of human nature.

• He may negotiate the deal for the chosen composer and/or songwriter/lyricist.

• He may negotiate the deal for preexisting songs from publishers, record companies and artists. The experienced music supervisor has relationships with song publishers and record companies and knows how to prioritize the money in negotiations. For instance, the filmmaker may select four songs that he desires to be placed in the film, one of which is crucially important to the project in a specific context, the other three merely important in the context of a general musical style. Although all four "first selections" may not be affordable because they are with different publishers, by negotiating with the publisher of the one important song, that publisher will probably give the filmmaker a bargain price on songs from his catalog that are stylistically similar to the less-important three. All of these negotiations must include provisions for future soundtrack CD/tape sales. The music supervisor may then negotiate with record companies about producing a CD of the film's sountrack.

- Throughout all of this, the music supervisor is mindful of the production company's publishing interests.

- During filming, he may view occasional dailies with the filmmaker and the composer and give input on the musical concept.

- He may help to some degree with temp track.

- He shepherds the score through the whole process of spotting, booking recording studios and scoring mixer, coordinating the budget with the music contractor, overseeing the music library, attending scoring sessions and dub, etc.

In short, the music supervisor should (1) give administrative support and creative input to the composer/filmmaker relationship for the underscore and (2) work directly with the filmmaker on the choice and acquisition of songs for the film. In the first function, providing support for the underscore portion of the film, the music supervisor has to retain a delicate balance between being supportive and not becoming intrusive—a tough job. The main creative link should always be between the composer and the filmmaker. The music supervisor best serves the film's interests by buttressing that relationship, helping to clarify issues when the composer and filmmaker get bogged down in communication problems, explaining budget realities to both parties, etc.

Hiring a music supervisor should be done early in preproduction to address musical considerations within the script; i.e., to see if the film's music budget is realistic for the size of the underscore ensemble and song purchases required and to coordinate any prerecords that may be needed prior to shooting. Choosing a music supervisor must be done with great care—the musical issues within a film can get extremely complex and experience is crucial.

A filmmaker might think of a music supervisor in terms of a musical casting director—after discussing musical concepts, he presents the filmmaker with many options regarding songs to be purchased and composers to be hired in a sort of distillation process.

Music supervisors have many different backgrounds. Some used to be working musicians, composers, or recording engineers. Others have been executives in the recording industry or have a business/legal background. Knowing the particular strengths of the music supervisors you're considering as they relate to your film may help you make the best choice.

Not every film requires the services of a music supervisor. If your film is a low-to-medium-budget project with a straight-ahead underscore and the need for only a couple of purchased songs, it would be best to employ the composer on a package deal for the underscore, then contract for the services of a music clearance company to acquire the rights to the songs. However, if the score is complicated for any reason (large orchestra budget and administration thereof, many songs to purchase, prerecorded dance numbers or songs being done on-camera, etc.), a music supervisor is well worth the expenditure.

DIFFERENCES BETWEEN INDEPENDENT SUPERVISORS AND STUDIO MUSIC DIRECTORS

There are only a few differences between the independent music supervisor and the studio music director. Primarily, the studio music director has a huge corporate support system at his disposal and delegates a lot of the duties to the music library, music clearance and legal departments, sound departments, in-house music editorial department, etc. This corporate structure allows him to work with the same music production team and studio executives time and time again, which can make for a smoother road for all concerned. Additionally, the studio music director may have the benefit of easy (and often less-expensive) access to the studio's recording arm, so hit songs and recording artists contracted to the company are more available to the film. And after the in-house resources have been combed through, the sheer volume of films produced at a major studio gives the studio music director an edge in negotiating with outside publishers and record companies for the use of songs from their catalog.

Often, studio directors hire independent music supervisors to help with certain in-house films, or they may work in coordination with independents who are supervising projects financed or distributed, but not actually produced, by the studio.

Composing for a film that has a qualified music supervisor on the team is a joy, for creative and logistical communication between composer and filmmaker is greatly facilitated—it can be a very smooth road for the composer, and he can concentrate on composing.

10
THE MUSIC EDITOR

The important role of the music editor is often not very visible, and filmmakers occasionally ask me if money could be saved by not hiring one. The answer is "no." In short, the music editor is the main link to the timing and placement of all music in the film and is worth every penny spent on his services.

Some projects may need prerecorded music to be played back during filming of scenes where dancers, singers, or instrumentalists are on the screen synching to that music track. It's the music editor's job to prepare the prerecorded music ahead of time with proper synch encoding, then attend the shoot to be sure the on-screen dancers or musicians are in proper synch, to coordinate technical matters with the camera or sound people, etc. Most music editors have had musical training at some point in their lives, and they can be a big help on the shoot. For instance, they are able to ensure that the actor faking to the prerecorded piano music isn't playing on the high notes when the playback track is sounding low notes. I cannot stress enough how crucial it is to have prerecords performed correctly by the actors and the sound/camera technicians. Otherwise, it can be an expensive fix in postproduction when the music, sound and visual elements don't line up properly. Even in a seemingly simple sequence in which the actors sing "For He's a Jolly Good Fellow" or a Christmas carol, having a music editor on line before and during the shoot can eliminate later editorial problems that may be insurmountable.

With that rare exception of prerecords, the first role of the music editor is usually to help build the music temp track using preexisting film music from CDs. When done in conjunction with the composer, it can be a very strong temp. As I mentioned before, having the composer help with the temp track (perhaps even using some music from other scores he's composed) can be an excellent way for the filmmaker and composer to communicate about the musical concept for the film. For the music editor to create a temp track without the input of the composer can create problems because all musical options may not be fully explored.

Secondly, the music editor is a crucial part of the music spotting session. He writes down the footage numbers at the beginning and end of each music cue, assigns all underscore and source cues a number according to their placement in the reels (first cue in the first reel is 1m1 or m11, second cue in first reel is 1m2 or m12, and so on), and tries to help the production team foresee any technical complications that may arise. At the end of the spotting session, the music editor totals the number of minutes of source and underscore music so that the composer, producer, music supervisor, and music contractor can begin to make informed decisions about the budget, size of orchestra (which dictates the size and cost of the recording studio), number of days required to record, etc.

Immediately following the spotting session, the music editor retires to his studio with a print or videotape of the locked film and begins to type up the timing notes for the composer. The timing notes (Example 2, page 26) are a precisely timed list of the events during that portion of the film where a music cue will occur. The composer uses these timings to ensure that the music exactly fits the action of the scene, whether he wants to hit or miss an event (a musical hit must occur within 2/10 of a second of the film event for proper synch). The music editor also types up a master log of all score and source music cues called "spotting notes" (Example 1, page 25), which helps all parties in postproduction and dub communicate coherently.

As the composer is writing, he may decide to begin or end a cue a few seconds earlier or later and ask the music editor to compute revised timing notes for that cue, then deliver them (by fax, modem, or messenger) to his studio. The film may even be recut a bit as the composer is working, and all timings will need to be revised, retyped, and sent to the composer so that he may make the necessary changes in the music.

As the composer completes the cues, the timing and tempo

information is relayed to the music editor (usually trough the transfer of computer MIDI files via email), who then prepares playback video for the music recording and subsequent dubbing session.

This preparation can include programming the computer to generate visual streamers on the playback monitor. A streamer is a diagonal line that takes two seconds to pass from the left side of the screen to the right and serves as a synch cue for the conductor and music editor. Generally, a yellow streamer signals for the warning clix to begin (a certain number of warning clix is specified by the composer so that the orchestra will hear a few beats of the proper tempo in their headphones before they actually begin to play). A green streamer signals the actual beginning of the cue, white or blue streamers are interior signals within the music cue and have various meanings, and a red streamer signals the end of the music cue. Drawing or computer-generating the streamers on film or videotape can take the music editor one to three days, depending on the complexity of the score.

During the time the composer is writing, the music editor is also preparing and "laying in"* songs or other prerecorded music that has been purchased. Sometimes the film footage of actors or dancers synching to prerecorded music hasn't been shot, synch-encoded, or cut properly by the film editor, so the music no longer fits the film. In this case, the music editor must spend time (sometimes a lot of time) cutting the piece of music so that it will fit the action on the film and still make musical sense. This problem usually occurs when the music editor wasn't brought onto the project soon enough and therefore wasn't able to coordinate the other production disciplines.

Prior to the recording session, the music editor and the composer make sure that the recording studio knows which tape format the production company prefers for the final mixed master. He also has to be sure to put the final synched music tracks on the proper tape format in preparation for the dub.

At the recording session, the music editor usually sits next to the composer with a computer or digital metronome and starts and stops the clix. He also keeps a running record of good and bad takes, of any splices that need to be made, of any mixing details

---

* When "laying in" music, the music editor places the music cues in exact synch on the film's music tracks in preparation for the dub.

to communicate to the music mixer at the dub, etc. If the composer and/or the filmmaker decide to make a change in the timing of the cue (a slightly different beginning or ending, for instance), the music editor helps the composer figure the timings and synch mathematics necessary to make sure that the music will still fit the picture. If other technical questions arise, the music editor and/or the scoring mixer will probably have the answer—or know how to get it.

After the recording session, the music editor places the finished music cues in their proper place in the music tracks in preparation for the dub, makes a list of that placement for the music mixer at the dub, then delivers it all to the dubbing stage. This is done in a "prelay session" for videotape. The music editor will probably be present at the dub to help sort out any problems and to be sure that all music tracks have been transferred cleanly and accurately. If the composer is unable to attend the dub, then the music editor often acts as the composer's advocate in that never-ending battle between sound effects and music. If the filmmaker wants to add, delete, or alter cues at any time after the recording session, the music editor makes those changes.

After the dub, the music editor assembles the music cue sheets, listing the title, length, writer, publisher, and usage of each music cue within the score (Example 7). The cue sheets are then sent to ASCAP and BMI by the production company or studio so that the performing rights royalties can be distributed properly. The composer should also be given a copy of the cue sheets for his records as ASCAP and BMI do make occasional errors in the survey of performances and subsequent money distribution, and the composer's discovery of these errors can benefit the production company/studio in receiving the proper publisher's royalties.

A note of caution here: Some music editors have compiled tape libraries of source music in which they own an interest. They sell these to the production company, then also reap financial benefits from writing and/or publishing royalties on the backend. Make sure that this isn't being done without your knowledge; you may not be getting a full range of options when choosing source music for your film.

The union that represents music editors is The Motion Picture and Videotape Editors Guild.

 UNIVERSAL TELEVISION

a division of Universal City Studios, Inc.
100 Universal City Plaza
Universal City, California 91608

MUSIC CUE SHEET

SERIES: MURDER, SHE WROTE - (1 HOUR)
PROD. NO: 62117
EPISODE TITLE: "NO ACCOUNTING FOR MURDER"

1ST U.S. AIR DATE: 3/22/87 - CBS
1ST CANADIAN AIR DATE: 3/20/87

| TITLE | PUBLISHER OR RIGHTS SECURED FROM | | USAGE |
	COMPOSER	PUBLISHER	
REEL I			
1. ACCOUNTING TEASER	David Bell (ASCAP)	MCA Music Publishing, A Div. of MCA, Inc. (ASCAP)	Ins.Bkg. :31
3. MURDER, SHE WROTE (THEME)(M.T.)	John Addison (ASCAP) - USA (PRS) - Rest of the World	"	" :46
3. NEW YORK, NEW YORK	Words: Fred Ebb Music: John Kander (BMI)	CBS Unart Catalogue (BMI)	" :50
4. NEW YORK, NEW YORK PLAYON	David Bell (ASCAP)	MCA Music Publishing, A Div. of MCA, Inc. (ASCAP)	" 1:16
5. BAG LADY	"	"	" :15
6. CONNIE RUNS	"	"	" :30
7. GHOST'S P.O.V.	"	"	" :19
REEL II			
8. HANDWRITING ON THE WALL	David Bell (ASCAP)	MCA Music Publishing, A Div. of MCA, Inc. (ASCAP)	Ins.Bkg. :17
9. HUMMING (NO TUNE)	Staff	------------------	Vis.Voc. :18

Example 7: Music cue sheet for an episode of *Murder She Wrote*, which is submitted to ASCAP and BMI. Performance royalties are dispensed based upon this information. [Courtesy of Universal Television.]

11
USE OF SONGS

Songs can be used as featured performances in Main Title or End Credit music, as part of the script (whether or not we see actors singing it on screen), or as source music that is emanating from a sound source on or off the screen (such as a radio, television, jukebox, live band). Two categories of songs can be used in a film: (1) preexisting songs (sheet music and recordings) or (2) original songs acquired by employing a composer and lyricist.

PREEXISTING SONGS

The music industry, especially the songwriting/recording industry, is extremely complex. Filmmakers are constantly surprised when they near the end of postproduction, begin shopping around for songs to use, and find themselves running into a buzzsaw of music publishers, music attorneys, high usage fees, restrictions on usage, etc. It's expensive and complicated, and if you don't think ahead, you could end up in a bad situation.

For instance, if your actors are singing a song on camera during a particular scene, don't assume that you can get the rights later. The rights to use the song may be prohibitively expensive or may not be granted for any price.

A true story: Once a upon a time, a production company made a film that climaxed with two teenage girls committing suicide together in one of their bedrooms. On the wall was a poster of a famous rock star the girls idolized, and the plan was to later dub in one of this rock star's songs as if it were emanating from the stereo in the bedroom. The scene was shot, and as the film was being edited, the production company began negotiations with the publisher and/or record company who owned the rock star's music. As is always done, the publisher and/or record company asked how the song was being used: the length of use, context within the picture, etc. When told of the scene, the publisher and/or record company broke off negotiations, saying something to the effect of, "Under *no* circumstances may you use *any* song of this rock star in conjunction with teen suicide. Furthermore, you may not use the poster with the rock star's image in such a scene." Needless to say, the entire scene had to be reshot without the poster on the wall.

For centuries, a prevalent attitude has been that music is free (or at least very cheap), that composers and lyricists exercise their talent as a hobby, that a work belongs to the public once it is written, that artists should give away their work for the publicity and exposure they'll receive. It's important to understand that the music business is complex, that a *lot* of money is at stake, that such intellectual property is a valuable commodity and is fiercely protected. Thinking ahead regarding the music will make your life much easier.

When using a preexisting song, you must acquire/negotiate two rights: the synchronization license and the master use license.

SYNCHRONIZATION LICENSE

The "synch license" is negotiated with the publisher(s) of the song. The publisher's identity will be on the record, CD, or sheet music. You will need to contact the publisher (this is usually done by the music supervisor, the music clearance department of the studio/production company, or an independent music clearance company) and describe the use of the song within the film, i.e., the length of the use, the context within the scene, how prominent (coming from a radio in the background or being sung on screen by an actor in a featured performance). The price will vary, of course, depending on whether you want a big hit song or a "throwaway" (a lesser-known cut by the same artist). The prices for the synch license can range from $1 for a song you purchase from your nephew's rock band to $200,000 for a current hit.

You now have the right to use the notes and lyrics of that song, but not the artist's recording of that song. In other words, if you've purchased the synch license from the publisher for the Beatles' tune *Yesterday* and want your composer to arrange it for piano solo in a restaurant or dance band at a high-school reunion, this is as far as you need to go. However, if you want to use the actual Beatles' recording of *Yesterday*, you must get the master use license.

MASTER USE LICENSE

The "master use license" for the original recording is negotiated with the record company who owns the master tapes. This can be the same amount of money as the synch fee. Not only must you pay the record company their fee, but all the artists on the recording must receive repayment of their original union wage for reuse (in current dollars). The record company is responsible for this, which is included in their fee. This holds true whether the recording is a single artist playing a piano solo or an entire orchestra—each musician gets repaid.

Once again, these negotiations are expensive and can take a lot of time. You may not be able to afford your first choice in songs and will need to discuss alternatives. This is where a good music supervisor or music clearance house can be invaluable. They've performed this task thousands of times and will be able to look at your budget and immediately tell you if your artistic choices can be fulfilled. They also know many ways to finagle deals. For instance, a publisher or record company may give you a break on the hit song you want if you'll agree to use a few of their lesser-known songs from their catalog in the film; this way they make money on the backend with the performing rights or CD sales of the soundtrack.

I strongly urge you to hire a qualified music supervisor or music clearance person long before the shoot begins to discuss these issues within your script.

ORIGINAL SONGS

Original songs can be written by the underscore composer collaborating with a lyricist, or they can be written by an independent songwriter/lyricist. Original songs can reflect deeper meaning and insight into characters/plots (e.g., *The Way We Were* by Marvin Hamlisch and Alan and Marilyn Bergman for the film of the same name and *Let the River Run* by Carly Simon for the film *Working Girl*). Original songs can speak directly to the heart of a film in ways that preexisting songs rarely can.

THE FUNCTION OF SONGS

Fairly early in the history of film, songs or themes that were written for movies began to win Oscars and make money outside the context of the film with radio play, record sales, and sheet music. One of the first of these was *Zip-a-Dee-Doo-Dah* from the Disney film *Song of the South*. At this time, most songs used in films were composed specifically for the purpose of making a dramatic statement; they weren't written with the primary intent of creating a hit outside the context of the film. Some themes that were written for successful films had lyrics added later for commercial performances (such as David Raksin's tune *Laura*, with lyrics by Johnny Mercer and Maurice Jarre's theme for *Dr. Zhivago*, which became the song *Somewhere My Love* with lyrics by Paul Francis Webster).

This evolved to the point where the film studio and record-company executives began to realize that quite a bit of income could be generated by placing preexisting hit songs within films. Deals were struck, money was made, and eventually the situation evolved to where it is today: songs being purchased and placed in films, not for artistic reasons, but because they might sell more soundtrack records/CDs. It's now to the point where film-soundtrack CDs that include songs which never appeared in the film are manufactured and sold! The power of the record companies within the film industry has become enormous; it's a bit of the tail wagging the dog.

Using preexisting hit songs for a flavor of the time and location in which the film takes place can sometimes be very effective (Martin Scorsese's *Goodfellas*), but they must be used with care. Remember that preexisting hit songs are very subjective, personal entities; the nostalgic hit song that has a positive association for *you* may be the same song that has a negative association for a member of the audience (i.e., it was the song playing on the radio as his fiancée called off the wedding).

Too often songs are used in today's films because filmmakers don't fully understand the possibilities of underscore, trusting that a composer will be able to compose original music appropriate for their film: often songs are "shoehorned" into a film for the wrong reasons. In this case, the filmmaker can't visualize the full impact of a scene without music and is hesitant to wait until an original underscore is written, so the rule becomes: When in doubt, buy a song! As I mentioned earlier, some music supervisors and music editors sell songs from their own catalog to the film, retaining the publishing performing rights so that they can benefit from royalties; when done with full knowledge and consent of the filmmaker, it's called "packaging" and can save the film money on the frontend.

The incorrect use of songs endangers the cohesiveness of film art. Instead of a two-hour dramatic statement, motion pictures often become bits of plot interspersed between MTV-like music videos.

In any case, try to include the underscore composer in decisions regarding the use of songs, for he may be able to find better, less expensive solutions.

12
ASCAP and BMI

Frequently, I encounter filmmakers who assume that these organizations are composers' unions and are to be avoided. Quite the contrary—they can be very helpful to the filmmaker and production company who understand their function.

ASCAP (American Society of Composers, Authors and Publishers) and BMI (Broadcast Music, Incorporated) are *not* composers' unions, but performing rights organizations.* ASCAP and BMI are the organizations that collect and disburse performance royalties to the composers, lyricists, and publishers who own the music. They collect money only from the venues that perform/play live or recorded music, such as television and radio stations, concert halls, ice rinks, restaurants and bars, companies who use soothing music in elevators or on the "hold" mode in their phone system, etc. Anybody who uses music by ASCAP or BMI writers to enhance their business must pay a licensing fee to these organizations.

Although payment options are available, for ease of accounting, most venues choose to pay a "blanket license fee" to ASCAP and BMI; the blanket license fee gives that venue the right to use any music by an ASCAP or BMI writer without having to negotiate a separate agreement each time a piece of music is performed. In the case of a television network, the annual blanket license fee would be in the millions of dollars; for a small bar or restaurant, probably a few hundred dollars.

The point I want to make here is that filmmakers or film studios never have to pay anything to ASCAP or BMI (unless they

---

* In fact, film composers do not have a union; the Composers and Lyricists Guild of America was broken by the studios in the early 1970s.

use canned music in their elevators and telephones). In fact, the studios or production companies belong to ASCAP and BMI as publishers and receive an equal amount of royalty income from these performing rights organizations as do the composers. Knowing this can help the filmmaker make a better deal with a composer. For instance, if the project doesn't have a big music budget, you can usually get the composer to agree to a smaller up-front fee in return for giving him part or all of the publisher's share of the performing royalties on the cue sheet (see Example 7, page 61) while retaining the copyright. Most composers are willing to take the risk with you and make a deal such as this.

Composers and lyricists usually belong to one organization or the other (occasionally switching if they feel that they can get more money, more personal attention, etc.). Publishers, especially the big ones in the recording or film industry, will typically belong to both; they usually use their ASCAP publishing arm when sharing a cue sheet with an ASCAP composer and their BMI publishing arm when sharing with a BMI composer.

ASCAP represents about 60% of works performed, BMI about 40%, with a smaller performing rights society, SESAC Inc.,* representing a very small portion. They are competitors and have different payment schedules for all types of performances.

To understand how this royalty disbursement system works, you must think of the royalty as being a 200% entity: 100% writer's share (which can be split among any number of people depending on how many composed or wrote lyrics for the piece of music) and 100% publisher's share (which can also be split among several entities). The publisher share can be bought or sold or negotiated away for various reasons (such as giving the composer a portion of the publishing royalties on a film score in exchange for a lower up-front fee). Refer to the cue sheet, Example 7, which is assembled by the music editor and submitted to ASCAP or BMI by the production company or studio so that the writers and publishers will be properly credited and paid. Be sure that the composer and lyricist get copies of the completed cue sheets for their files; in future years, they may discover accounting errors in their

---

* Decades ago, SESAC was the acronym for Society of European Stage Authors and Composers, but now the acronym has become the complete, official name of the company.

royalty statements from ASCAP or BMI, which could result in financial benefits for your company or publisher.

* * *

ASCAP and BMI "survey" or sample most of the media or venues that perform music written or owned by their members. They have computer linkups with television programming services for information on what shows are airing on what network, local or cable television stations and systems. In the radio area, programming is either taped or logs of airplay are submitted by the stations. Some licensed areas are surveyed on a census basis (100% count) with others on a sample. That information is processed and given a credit value (i.e., one minute of music on network prime time is worth more than one minute of a daytime airing, which is worth more than one minute on a small cable broadcast, etc.); this is translated to a dollar value and payment is made three calendar quarters after the broadcast. The dollar value of performance credits varies from quarter to quarter depending on how much money the performing rights organization collected during that time and the number of performances in each licensed area. Checks to writers and publishers are disbursed each quarter.

ASCAP and BMI also have reciprocal agreements with the performing rights organizations in other countries so that money flows back and forth when an ASCAP or BMI work is performed overseas and vice versa.

To join ASCAP or BMI, you must have written or be the publisher of music that is performed in any media licensed by those performing rights organizations.

ASCAP and BMI can also be of assistance if your production company has exhausted all avenues in tracking down the publisher or composer/lyricist on an obscure piece of music you'd like to use. Usually this information is listed on the album, CD, or sheet music or can be acquired through one of the many music clearance houses in Los Angeles (who will also help you negotiate the rights); the need for you to call ASCAP or BMI for this information will be rare.

Addresses and phone numbers for these performing rights societies may be found in the reference section at the back of this book.

13
Musicians' Union (American Federation of Musicians)

Most U.S. filmmakers and composers are based in Los Angeles and I write from that perspective, remaining as objective as possible. Traditionally, the film scoring here sets the standard for the world.

As I mentioned before, composers do not have a labor union. However, virtually all of the composers working in mainstream film and television in Hollywood belong to the AFM as conductors and orchestrators. It's in this capacity that they receive pension and health benefits. However, this situation can become sticky sometimes because most composers wear three hats: (1) owner/president of a music corporation/business, (2) freelance composer/employee of that business, and (3) member of the musicians' union. Needless to say, these three entities can come into conflict as they sometimes have different interests at heart, especially when writing music under a "package deal" contract (more about this in Chapter 14).

On the whole, the union rules under which the musicians work during recording sessions are fair for both sides. The music contractor, although a member of the union, is a referee of sorts making sure that the musicians are protected from exploitation by filmmakers and that filmmakers are protected from padded time cards, etc. Go out of your way to foster a good relationship with the music contractor,—he and the composer will do all they can to save you money and time on the recording stage.

Although the rules and pay scales for AFM musicians are complex, below are a few basics that may be helpful to know as you try to communicate with the composer and music contractor.

Musicians are usually hired in blocks of three- or six-hour

minimums with overtime scales for each. The basic scale for a three-hour call under the Motion Picture/TV Film agreement* is currently (1994) $202.71 per salary for an orchestra of thirty five or more (this figure includes 4% vacation pay for independent productions). The rate is slightly higher for smaller ensembles; the union likes to think of it as giving a discount for using more players. Add to that FICA, SDI, health and welfare benefits, etc., and it's a good idea to figure just under $300.00 per salary per three hours. Overtime runs $16.89 per salary for every fifteen minutes for the first hour (this is the basic scale prorated). The costs go up during the second overtime hour to 150% of basic scale, prorated in fifteen minute units.

Several musicians in the orchestra will get more than base scale. If they are the Concertmaster, important principal player in a section, or the "top call" people, they'll get double scale or a guaranteed instrumental "double" (note that these are two different things, "double scale" being self-explanatory).

An instrumental "double" occurs when a musician is proficient on more than one instrument and is asked to play that second or third (or fourth, fifth, sixth, etc.) instrument during a recording session in which he is also playing his primary instrument. For instance, when a flute player also plays a piccolo or an alto flute in a few passages written by the composer, he will get 50% in addition to base scale for that second instrument, another 20% in addition to base scale will be added to that if a third and subsequent instruments are called for. Other common "doublers" include synthesists with multiple keyboards or acoustic piano, trumpet players doubling flugelhorn or high trumpets (such as piccolo trumpet), reed players who play several instruments (clarinet, bass clarinet, alto sax, tenor sax, etc.), percussionists who play several instruments, guitarists who play both acoustic and electric, etc. This system is very fair, for although the instruments are usually related, they are different disciplines and require hundreds of hours of extra practice to master them. The doubles and double scales can add

---

* In the summer of 1994, the AFM and the Alliance of Motion Picture and Television Producers (AMPTP) agreed on an experimental two-year contract for low-budget motion pictures that will lower the musicians' basic three-hour wage scale from $202.71 to $135.00. This only applies to motion pictures with production budgets of less than $12 million. This new agreement will also apply on a "case-by-case" basis to motion pictures made for basic cable television, motion pictures initially released on videocassette, and long-form television movies.

another 20% to 30% to the base scale, per salary budget. However, it ultimately saves money—if only a few selected musical passages need another instrumental color, the doubling system makes it unnecessary to hire another person at full salary.

"Overdubbing" occurs when, after recording one instrumental part of music, the tape is rewound and the musician records another separate, distinct part. For this, he's paid another full salary.

Other union musicians to be paid are orchestrators and copyists whose page counts are converted to an hourly wage formula for computing taxes and benefits.

SCORING OVERSEAS OR DOMESTICALLY NON-UNION

It's important to note that a composer who is a member of the AFM can only legally record (including orchestrate and conduct) outside of the U.S. if the film was shot/produced abroad. However, most composers will record in alternate venues as long as the quality is good.

In the opinion of composers with whom I've spoken, the three locations in the world that offer the best musicians and recording facilities for achieving that distinctive, robust, flawless filmmatic sound are Los Angeles, New York, and London; in my informal poll, Los Angeles seems to have a slight edge over the other two. In general, Hollywood composers feel more comfortable keeping the work in town because they know the players, the orchestrators and copyists, the scoring mixers/recording engineers, the recording stages, etc.; these long-standing relationships can have a positive impact on the quality of the score.

Although scores can always be produced cheaper in another country or with non-union musicians in the U.S., the maxim "you get what you pay for" holds true for music scoring. Although union musicians in the U.S. and London cost more per hour, they make fewer mistakes, which means fewer bad takes. In the long run, this saves money. In addition, the extremely high caliber of performance (expressiveness, intonation, quick sightreading ability, etc.) and stylistic versatility usually makes scoring union in Los Angeles, New York, and London the best options; even the second- and third-string musicians give a wonderful performance.

After figuring the costs of flying a half dozen production people overseas (a couple of producers, a director, a composer, a music editor, an orchestrator, sometimes even a scoring mixer), paying hotel bills and per diems, etc., overseas scoring doesn't always save enough money to warrant the risk of dealing with the unpredictable quality of foreign studios and orchestras. Although many composers have had good experiences with European orchestras, just as many have been disappointed; some have even returned to Los Angeles and rerecorded the entire soundtrack. For some, going overseas places too many unknowns into the equation.

The money saved by going overseas or scoring non-union domestically is on the backend. Most of the European or U.S. non-AFM orchestras are a buyout—no repayments are ever made for new use or supplemental markets. This is the major reason that production companies go overseas or use non-union musicians.

"New use" payments are owed to the AFM musicians when a recording is used in another category or production. For instance, if a cut from a record album/CD is used in a film or television show, the musicians must be repaid 100% of their salaries in the scale of the new medium.

"Supplemental market" payments are owed to the musicians when the project is sold to another market (i.e., feature film to video, television movie to feature distribution, feature film to airlines, etc.). Whatever entity owns the project (production company or studio/distributor) and receives income from a backend sale will owe the AFM 1.5% of adjusted gross (adjusted gross is approximately 60% of gross) from that sale.* That money is then distributed by the AFM to the musicians who played the recording sessions for that soundtrack. These backend payments rarely come to more than $50,000 to $75,000 *over the life* of a major motion-picture hit, and no money is paid unless and until the film makes money in these supplemental markets.

---

* Adjusted gross is computed after deducting the hard costs of preparing the film for another market (such as the purchase and duplication of millions of videocassettes); normal production expenses such as accounting, secretarial, and office supplies are not included in this deduction.

ALTERNATIVE SCORING VENUES

Overseas

London: This has been one of the most popular alternative cities for film scoring since the early 1980s. This is due to the fact that musicians' salaries are less than in the U.S. (it's particularly economical when a favorable currency rate is in effect) and that the payment is a buyout—no fringe benefits are paid and no backend payments are owed. Like New York and Los Angeles, London offers an enormous pool of musical talent.

Ireland: Dublin has become a favorite in recent years with Hollywood producers for two reasons mentioned above: a favorable currency exchange rate and a buyout payment. Quality of performance and recording here is good as long as the first-string musicians are available.

Munich: An alternate that was growing in popularity in the early 1990s. However, the depth of talent wasn't sufficient, and if the first-string players weren't available, the second- and third-string couldn't provide top-notch results. A couple of motion-picture scores done there were of such poor quality that they had to be rerecorded in Los Angeles; few scores are taken there anymore.

Budapest: A composer who scored there recently rated the musicians as excellent and the recording facilities good. However, the economy is such that the musicians cannot afford top-notch instruments and the sound suffered greatly. He won't record there again for this reason.

North America

Some producers hear through the grapevine that money can be saved by scoring in Canada, Seattle, or other North American cities. This is true, but these options also share many of the same problems as scoring overseas.

Canada (primarily Toronto and Vancouver): The AFM is also the union in Canada, so similar rules for backend payments apply. The monetary savings come from a favorable currency exchange rate and lower fees for synth rentals, cartage, mixers, tape, and studios. A music supervisor I know did a recent comparison on scoring a television movie in Los Angeles vs. Toronto. After taking into consideration flying, hotels, and per diem for all concerned, the savings were a little under $3,000 on a $75,000 Movie-of-the-Week music budget. As you can see, it may not be worth the hassle.

Seattle: The Seattle Symphony is an excellent orchestra that recently decertified from the AFM and formed its own union. The musicians cost less all the way around, but once again, the issue of depth must be considered; if the first-string players aren't available, it's not easy to put together a top-notch orchestra. The orchestra and recording facilities have produced great-sounding CDs of classical concert works but are not set up well for film scoring; usually a mobile studio in a truck is parked next to the concert hall or a recording booth is set up in the basement. Needless to say, this makes for inconvenient communication and playback.

Salt Lake City: This has been a hotbed of union controversy in recent years because of the "right-to-work" status of Utah; the musicians there have drawn many film scores away from Los Angeles with lower hourly rates and no backend payments. Quality suffers there and some composers who have recorded there refuse to return for that very reason. Both Seattle and Salt Lake are such controversial situations that many composers won't score in either place because of their union loyalties.

* * *

These are but a few of the many scoring situations around the world. Things are always in a state of flux, and the words I've written about these scoring venues may no longer be true in the near future, but it gives you a baseline for discussion with your composer.

The bottom line regarding this global hopscotching in music scoring has nothing to do with quality and very little to do with frontend payments (a lower hourly rate is meaningless if the session requires many more hours of recording time to get a flawless score). The real issue is the backend payments owed to union musicians. These rarely amount to much money, even on a major motion-picture hit and, in my opinion, are certainly worth the expenditure when getting the highest quality performance available.

The musicians perform a creative function and deserve repayments for supplemental markets and new use. Their creative contributions to the notes in the score are much the same as the creative contributions that actors bring to a script. The quality of performance is what makes the score come alive. The large number of excellent musicians currently living in Los Angeles, New York, and London is probably the greatest collection of musical talent that the world has ever known; much of the reason that so many musicians have settled in these cities is due to the recording/film industry and the monies they can receive under the AFM contracts. It's a resource of talent that must be protected and nurtured on a long-term basis. Okay, I'll get off my soapbox now.

14
PACKAGE DEALS

The "package deal" composer contract became prevalent in the mid-1980s. It's used in some medium-budget films and virtually all low-budget films and television movies and series. In the package deal, a composer is given a set amount of money and is responsible for the administering, producing, accounting, and composing of the music score.* He receives "x" number of dollars, then hands the production company a finished master tape at the end of the scoring process, pocketing whatever is left over as his salary. Until the package deal arrived on the scene, composers were paid a fee, then the studio or production company took care of all administrative/budget work. In that case, if some event outside the composer's control caused the music score to go overbudget, those few extra hundreds or thousands of dollars were easily covered by the studio; that same overbudget cost to today's composer on a package deal can be disastrous, and he will cut corners or pad the budget to avoid losing money. Needless to say, when working on a package deal, the composer spends a lot of time and energy dealing with monetary/administrative issues rather than creative issues. Package deals are often not in the best interests of the film, the filmmaker, or the composer, but are probably here to stay, and most composers have become adept at making them work.

The only people who are guaranteed to benefit from a package deal are the production company budget chiefs who win corporate points for staying within the budget (and who sometimes refuse to increase the budget no matter what happens dur-

* There are companies that will do the administration, accounting, payroll, etc., for a fee, but that means that somebody else is taking another piece of the music budget.

ing the music production process) and some composers' agents who are now getting 10% to 15% commission on the gross package amount vs. 10% to 15% on only the composers' net fees, as was the case before package deals. In a package deal, these agents are making a lot more money for doing essentially the same amount of work as they would on a simple fee contract. Some agents have found an equitable balance by commissioning only 7% on the gross package-deal amount. Whatever the commission may be, remember to mentally deduct that amount immediately—in reality, your $100,000 music-package budget is now only worth $85,000 (figuring 15% commission) to $93,000 (figuring 7% commission). Your musical vision and discussions with your composer must be based on these revised figures.

The most workable scenario for a package deal is when the whole score is done in a home-synthesizer/recording studio and the project contains a predictable amount of music (such as a television episode). In this case, the composer has complete control of the situation. As soon as the score is taken to an outside studio with even a small instrumental ensemble, too many unexpected, uncontrollable events can put the composer overbudget. These events include the recording studio breaking down, a musician or his equipment showing up late or not getting to the date at all due to scheduling error, accident, sudden illness, etc.

As a compromise for scores that aren't completely synthesized, some high-end composers are able to make a package deal for that part of the score that is done in their home-synthesizer studio, then the studio/production company picks up the tab for any orchestral/acoustic "sweetening" done later at an outside recording studio. Note that home synthesizers do not necessarily save time and money—the composer not only writes the music, but then must perform all the parts with computer programming, synthesizers, and recording equipment (see Chapter 16 for more on this).

Most package-deal contracts have exclusions in them stipu-
lating that the composer isn't responsible for:

1) Music editors
2) Mag stock and transfers
3) Licensing of music not composed by the composer
4) Reuse, new use, supplemental-market fees, and any
   other residual type payments generated under the
   AFM agreement
5) Rescoring or rerecording required for creative reasons
   outside control of the composer after delivery of the
   master tape
6) Lyricist- and vocalist-related expenses
7) Sideline musician expenses (those musicians who appear on camera)
8) Prerecords (see Glossary)

There may also be restrictions on the maximum number of
minutes of score allowed under the package-deal agreement; if
more minutes of music are required, the extra cost of musicians,
studio, engineer, copying, recording tape, etc., will be picked up
by the studio or production company.

As a general rule of thumb, the music budget should be 1.5%
to 2.5 % of the total budget of the film (depending on the number of songs to be purchased). Take, for example, the average cost
of a television movie or low-to-middle-budget feature film with
thirty minutes of music: If a small acoustic ensemble is required
(ten to forty musicians), the package-deal budget should be somewhere between $45,000 and $80,000. If the score is done completely electronically in a home-synthesizer studio, the figures will
be approximately $25,000 to $50,000. A one-hour television episode should be $12,000 to $35,000 depending on the number of
musicians required and amount/type of music required. Quite
frankly, anything less than these minimum figures is inappropri-
ate unless the entire production crew has also taken a big cut in
pay and/or the publisher's share of performance royalties are as-
signed to the composer on the cue sheets as added compensa-
tion. Please see Chapter 15 for more details about music budgets.
    Using the package deal for a project requiring the use of an

acoustic instrumental ensemble or orchestra often doesn't serve the best interests of the film—the composer should be composing, not doing administrative work such as booking studios, recording engineers, music librarians, copyists, payroll service, and worrying that the filmmaker may put the recording session into serious overtime with lots of discussion and changes (the money for which comes out of the composer's pocket unless he has padded the budget to protect himself).

Package-deal budgets are almost always given a dollar figure before production begins, long before anybody knows what kind of music is needed (synthesized, acoustic, or a combination of the two), how many minutes of music are in the film, the time schedule for composing, how much source music or songs are needed, etc. Much too often, the budgets are unrealistic because they're put together by people who simply don't understand the complexities of creating a music score (they haven't read this book yet!). Furthermore, a production company will occasionally show zero flexibility, even when it becomes obvious that the music budget is inadequate. This means that the filmmaker's musical vision is often not fully realized unless the composer puts most or all of the budget into the score, thereby leaving himself little or nothing for a salary with only the hope that the filmmaker will be a repeat customer in the future. The package deal has caused too many composers to take a financial beating (sometimes going in the red) trying to meet the expectations of the filmmaker. If the music budget must be a package deal, be sure that it's a reasonable budget for the type and amount of music needed. An inadequate budget will often result in an inadequate score.

The package deal sometimes creates a barrier between the composer and filmmaker. When the filmmaker relates his musical vision in initial discussions, the composer wants nothing more than to say "yes, let's do it!"; but when the composer (as owner of his music business/corporation) has to repeatedly say "no, that's not possible due to budgetary restrictions," he is put in an awkward position and becomes the filmmaker's "enemy." There may even be suspicions on the part of the filmmaker that the composer is padding his pocket and not spending enough on the score (whether it be out of greed or as insurance against surprises). Rather than contracting the composer for a package deal, consider giving the composer a fee for his services and let the production company be responsible for the administration of the music-scoring budget. The filmmaker and composer should be allies in the creative process; it's the job of the studio executives or producers to say "no" and place limitations on the filmmaker's musical dreams.

* * *

Bottom line: Package deals are workable when a home-studio synthesizer or small acoustic ensemble score is called for, but when an acoustic/orchestral score is recorded in a commercial studio, it's usually better for all concerned if the composer is paid a fee for the score and the music budget and administration remains in control of the production company or studio.

15
MUSIC BUDGETS

This is a difficult chapter to write because many, many variables influence a music budget—most of which aren't even known until postproduction. The style of music (action vs. romantic), the instrumentation (electronic vs. acoustic), the amount of music, number and type of songs to be purchased, etc., all play a huge factor. The budget figures given below are very general. However, as stated earlier, a good general rule of thumb is that the music budget should be 1.5% to 2.5% of the total film budget.*

If the score requires using an electronic and/or acoustic ensemble in a commercial studio, there are costs outside of musicians' salaries to be aware of. When large instruments are trucked to the recording studio (harp, percussion, trunks full of synthesizer or guitar equipment), there are "cartage" charges. Most of these instruments are stored in warehouses and are trucked to the date by a cartage company, unpacked, set up, plugged in, tested, then broken down and returned to the warehouse or transported to the next recording studio when the date is over. These charges can be between $150 and $350 per musician. Rental fees of $200 to $400 can also be charged for percussion instruments and large synthesizer setups. Other non-musician charges include the payroll company, the recording studio, the scoring mixer, technicians, recording tape, piano tuning, video lockup, Dolby cards, etc.

Although it's generally assumed that money can be saved by doing a score completely electronically, this is often not the case as the hours of computer/synthesizer programming and recording add up very quickly on top of the cost of composing. Although

* This has fallen from music budgets being 3% to 5% of the total production budgets for films made forty or fifty years ago.

there is a savings when the project is a low-budget one and a young, entry level (rather desperate) composer is willing to bust his chops in his home-synth studio doing a package deal for a credit, the middle- and high-budget projects don't save much money when done electronically because the high-end composers and synthesists charge full fare for their time, computer/synthesizer programming, cartage of electronics to a recording studio, equipment rentals, several doubles or double and triple scale, etc.

A good example of this is a comparison of the costs to produce the scores for the films *Witness* and *Out of Africa* (excluding composer fees), both done in 1984-85. *Witness* was a totally electronic score, employed five synthesists (including their equipment rentals and cartage) for five days and cost about $150,000. *Out of Africa* was totally orchestral, employed over ninety musicians for three days, and cost almost exactly the same.

Composers and studio musicians who own extensive collections of synthesizers and electronics have a fortune invested in that equipment, and they are constantly updating—pieces of gear become obsolete quickly. Although the traditional acoustic string, wind, and brass instruments need occasional repair or maintenance, it's nothing compared to the operating costs of the electronic setups of synthesists, guitarists, and percussionists (remember, you're helping to pay for all of the expenses that go toward keeping an electronic rig in current, operating condition). However, it would be fair to say that, in recent years, synthesized underscore costs have not been rising as quickly as they had in the past due to better equipment and computer software.

Below are some figures and guidelines that may help you estimate music budgets for upcoming projects.

These numbers (1994 dollars) are for the underscore only and can vary widely due to many factors, but they represent a point of departure for discussion.

LOW-BUDGET FEATURE FILM

Usually, this situation means finding an entry-level composer who needs the credit for his résumé, then contracting for a package-deal score produced in his home-synthesizer studio. The job will take three to six weeks to finish and will cost $20,000 to $50,000.

It might even be possible to include a couple of acoustic instruments in the score. By producing the whole score in a home studio, money is saved in expenses such as a commercial recording studio, scoring mixer, orchestration, music copying, payroll, etc. Remember that you can also save up-front costs by giving the composer at least 50% of the publisher's performing rights so that he can make it up on the backend.

"Low-budget" does not automatically mean that an electronic score is the only possibility. Many excellent scores have been composed using small acoustic ensembles, sometimes with a bit of synthesizer instrumentation included (Elmer Bernstein's score to *My Left Foot* or Gary Chang's score to *A Shock to the System*). This, in fact, "separates the men from the boys" as it requires top-notch composing ability to write for a small instrumental group.

MEDIUM-BUDGET FEATURE FILM OR TELEVISION MOVIE

If electronic, the score will probably be composed/performed by a more established composer in a fairly high-end home-synthesizer studio plus a couple of studio musicians (who are also more-established and more expensive). This should also be done on a package deal and will cost in the neighborhood of $50,000 to $150,000.

Once the decision is made to use an ensemble that is mostly acoustic or a combination of electronic and acoustic, the budget becomes more complicated as studio time, recording mixer, copying, payroll, etc., get factored into the equation. The cost range on this sort of film would be approximately $50,000 to $300,000. I've chosen this category to give a detailed breakdown of costs to demonstrate that the production of the music score is a complex, expensive item in the making of a film. You can extrapolate these numbers up or down depending on your particular situation.

The number of minutes of music is a major factor in the budget; for this discussion, we'll assume that the project is a Movie-of-the-Week drama with an average of thirty to forty minutes of music (which should take about a day and a half—or nine scoring hours—to record, assuming that there aren't too many discussions, playbacks, and musical changes made while the orchestra/band is on the clock).

We'll also assume that the orchestra will be thirty-five musicians (remember, that's thirty-five musicians, not thirty-five salaries; the total number of salaries will be higher due to double scale for contractor and conductor, music sound consultant,* instrumental doubles, scale and a half for principals and soloists, etc.). This hypothetical budget is for an orchestra of a few wind players, harp, piano/synthesizer, plus full string section (violins, violas, 'cellos, contrabasses).

If a score has a lot of chase or adventure music in it, the costs will go up—increased difficulty means that more studio/mixer/musician time is needed to get a good take, and the orchestration and copying costs will also rise because fast music requires composing many more notes.

Remember: This budget is a ballpark figure only. More than giving cost breakdowns, it's here to demonstrate the complexity of producing a music score.

In preparing this book, the original budget estimate for the project was around $56,000 (excluding the composer's fee). However, just as this book was going to press, the AFM ratified a new low-budget agreement which lowers the cost of musicians, orchestrators, copyists, conductor, and contractor by about 30%. This new agreement applies to motion pictures with production budgets of less than $12 million. The agreement will also apply, on a "case-by-case" basis, to motion pictures made for basic cable television, motion pictures released initially released on videocassette, and long-form television movies. The following budget reflects this new agreement and totals only $40,455.

---

* Known by several titles (booth supervisor or music sound consultant), this person sits in the recording booth next to the scoring mixer with a set of scores and helps cue the scoring mixer for solos or other musical events necessary to get the the mix right. Usually, this person has also orchestrated the music for the composer and is very familiar with the musical concept.

Musicians	$ 18,225
(inc. contractor, conductor, music sound consultant)	
Fringe benefits	2,790
(pension + Health & Welfare)	
Music copying	4,000
Fringe benefits for copyists	800
Orchestration	3,500
Fringe benefits for orchestrators	600
Payroll taxes	3,860
(15% of base wages of $25,725)	
Payroll service fees*	1,030
(4% of above base wages and benefits)	
Copying supplies, messengers	400
1 synthesizer cartage	350
1 synthesizer rental	400
1 harp cartage	250
Scoring mixer	750
(9 hours + 1 hour setup)	
Recording studio @ $200 per hour	2,000
(9 hours + 1 hour setup)	
Recording tape (24-track, 4-track, DAT)	600
Transfer costs	300
Video linkup, rental of Dolby SR cards, piano tuning, etc.	600
TOTAL	$ 40,455

* Music payroll percentages are usually a bit higher than found in other areas of film-making due to the unique complexities involved.

Add to this amount the composer's fee which is $20,000 to $30,000 for a television movie and $30,000 to $100,000 for a medium-budget feature.

IMPORTANT NOTE! Many of the costs listed above do not change much when using a smaller instrumental ensemble: studio, scoring mixer, recording tape, video linkup, Dolby card rental, piano tuning, synth rental, equipment cartage, and transfer costs may be approximately the same. Even the music copying will be similar—copying one violin part costs approximately the same whether it's played by one violinist or twenty violinists (duplicating and collating one hand-copied violin part for the specified number of violinists will only double the cost, not multiply it by twenty times that of the original).

HIGH-BUDGET FEATURE FILM

The music production expenses for a high-budget film can reach $400,000. Large recording studios and large orchestras with four or five days of recording can accumulate expenses quickly. Add to that composer fees of $200,000 to $400,000 for high-budget feature films and the total budget can reach $1,000,000 or more.

* * *

As you can see, this is all very complex. Good, experienced music supervisors and music contractors are worth their weight in gold as they help you figure all of this out. Don't skimp on the music budget. A well-composed, well-performed, well-produced music score will enhance your film immeasurably.

16
SYNTHESIZED OR ACOUSTIC?

This is often regarded by most people to be an either/or proposition. Not true. Most film and television scores use a combination of acoustic instruments and synthesizers. It's best when the synthesizer is used as just another color in the composer's musical palette; this is a wonderful addition to the world of music when in the hands of someone who understands its function and unique character. However, the synthesizer is at its worst when used to duplicate acoustic/orchestral sounds for the purpose of replacing live musicians. This is much more than a moral issue (it's an accepted fact of life by the acoustic musicians that the new sounds of the synthesizer means less work for them). Replicating the depth and expressiveness of most acoustic instruments on synthesizer just isn't possible—it doesn't sound as good. This is equivalent to the visual difference between videotape and 35mm film.

A "synthesizer" is an instrument that generates sound electronically. Remember the high whistling sound that used to emanate from the old radios when dialing between stations? A synthesizer is based on the same principle but with many refinements. Different synth sounds are created by altering the shape of the basic sound wave (sine wave, sawtooth wave, etc.) and manipulating the overtones or harmonics (which is what gives all sounds their distinctive colors). Since it isn't possible to synthetically duplicate the sound of an acoustic instrument, the research and development people at the synthesizer companies came up with "digital sampling" to get closer to the real thing.

Digital sampling *is* the real thing in a sense. It's the digital recording of a sound (usually a single note) with all of the dozens of overtones intact. It's similar to recording a sound on a snip-

pet of standard audio recording tape and being able to play it over
and over at different speeds (i.e., different pitches). The digital
sampler makes it possible to access the original sampled snippet
of sound and manipulate it in a myriad of ways to create something new, such as transposing a flute sound into the tuba register, for instance. With sampling, the note retains the same overtones each time it is played. There's no variation in the overtones
as there would be with an acoustic instrument playing the same
pattern of notes. This variation in color is what makes music musical (like the artistic differences between a factory-made rug and
a handmade rug). However, sometimes this lack of variation or
human expressiveness is the desired result and works beautifully.

The synthesizers and samplers are initiated (triggered) by an
electronic impulse that comes from an electronic piano keyboard,
a computer that has been programmed by an electronic piano keyboard or standard computer keyboard, an electronic drum or
percussion pad (struck by a stick or mallet), a special sequencer,
an electronic valve instrument (EVI), electronic wind instrument
(EWI),* or an electric guitar or electric bass with a special pickup
on the body.

One composer who uses synthesizer well is Mark Isham. He
has a complete grasp of both electronic and acoustic musical instruments and makes excellent use of them separately or in combination. As I mentioned in a previous chapter, his score to *Never
Cry Wolf* is a good example of combining synthesized and acoustic
sounds. The plaintive, warm, soulful sounds of the solo bassoon
complemented the icy, pure tones of the synthesizer very well.

The score to *Never Cry Wolf* was composed over ten years ago
and, even though the synthesized sounds are now a bit dated, the
score still holds up because it was specific and well-composed for
the limitations of the instruments; the electronic parts would sound
awkward played by acoustic instruments and vice versa. Composing for the limitations of the instrument is analogous to the professional athlete who "plays within his abilities" (as the sports

---

* The EVI and EWI are sticks about eighteen inches in length and a couple of inches
in diameter and function as breath controllers that trigger the synthesizers and samplers. Keyed like a traditional woodwind instrument (EWI) or a three-valved brass instrument (EVI), the player is able to give the synthesizer notes human expressiveness
(which is difficult with the other triggering mechanisms mentioned above) by blow-
ing into the mouthpiece.

commentators are so fond of saying); if a smallish football quarterback repeatedly tries to bull his way up the middle as a fullback would, there's going to be a problem. Each family of acoustic or electronic instruments has its strengths and weaknesses.

In the following paragraphs, I'll try to articulate the drawbacks to the home-synthesizer studio; it's not always the panacea to the filmmaker's time and budget limitations that one may assume.

Rarely does one factory preprogrammed synthesizer/sampler sound possess satisfactory sonic depth, richness, and expressiveness. Creating one good sound often requires locking three or four synth/samplers together and shaping the attack, sustain, and decay contours so that they blend together. If the composer has enough synth/sampler machines tied to his computer, he's able to program the computer software to play all or most of a cue in one pass into the recording equipment. However, in some cases, the sounds must be layered onto multitrack tape beginning with a track of time code for synch, then making multiple passes recording one to three tracks at a time. If a couple acoustic instruments are to be included in the score, then they must be put down on tape in separate passes.* Naturally, it's not practical for the filmmaker to be present for most of this process, so when the filmmaker checks in occasionally and requests changes, that alteration can mean anything from an easy adjustment in the mix to starting the whole process all over again. Even if enough synth/samplers are available to make the recording in one pass, minor changes can require large amounts of time as each sound may need to be reshaped slightly, then brought back into sonic balance.

In most cases, making these same changes with an acoustic ensemble of any size is much easier. For instance, if a filmmaker's request for music alteration requires that two measures of music are cut from the middle of an orchestral cue, the conductor dictates that change to the musicians, who cross out those measures

---

* Remember that all of this is taking place after the composer has written the score. In times past, composing and conducting the orchestra were the extent of the composer's responsibilities. Today, the home-synthesizer-studio writer must be a composer, performer, recording engineer, computer programmer, synth/sampler programmer, music contractor, copyist, electronic technician, acoustician, etc. This can become such an enormous amount of work that the composer's primary function—composing—can get shortchanged.

on their written part. Some tempo adjustments are calculated by the composer/conductor to ensure that less music will still fit the length of the cue, then the orchestra plays the altered cue onto tape. The elapsed time for all of this is probably five minutes. That same change in a home-synthesizer studio can take up to an hour or two.

As I mentioned in Chapter 15 regarding music budgets, film-makers often automatically assume that a low-budget film can only have a synthesized score. This is not always the answer—many excellent low-budget films have been scored with a small acoustic ensemble. For example, Gary Chang's score to *A Shock to the System* featured a string quartet combined with synthesizers, Mark Isham's scores to *Trouble in Mind* and *The Moderns* used small ensembles of acoustic instruments plus synthesizer, as did Elmer Bernsteins' score to *My Left Foot*. A talented, trained composer can create superb music (both electronic and acoustic) with very limited resources. Make the choice between synthesized and/or acoustic music for artistic reasons and create a film score that will sound good today and for decades in the future.

17
FINAL THOUGHTS

The main point I hope to make with this book is that the production of a film score is a complex process that involves hiring and scheduling a veritable army of musicians, copyists, orchestrators, scoring mixer, recording stages (with their technicians, projectionists, tape, microphones, and other specific recording equipment), instrument cartage/rental, music contractor, musicians' payroll service, music editor, song licensing, etc. *These things require time and money!* Organizing all of this plus having creative meetings with the filmmaker can sometimes leave the composer with little time left over for the actual composing. Anything the filmmaker can do to give the composer adequate time, communication, or money will help (remember that more time can often solve problems inherent with too little money in the music budget).

As my colleagues like to say:

> Good and fast does not equal cheap,
> Good and cheap does not equal fast,
> Cheap and fast does not equal good.

18
QUICK REFERENCE
(OR THE SHORT ROAD TO
CINEMATIC/MUSICAL BLISS)

This chapter is designed to act as a quick refresher course for when you're in the middle of a project and don't have the time to reread the entire book.

Most important point: *The scoring process takes time and money. Plan ahead and don't skimp!*

The Function of Underscore (Chapter 1)

Film music can play with the action in a scene, play obliquely, play the subtext, show greater depth in character and drama than is apparent, play against the action in a scene.

Music may help but cannot save a bad picture.

Choosing the Composer (Chapter 2)

Hire a composer as soon as possible—no later than the beginning of the rough cut.

Hire the composer by continuing a preexisting personal relationship, listening to demo CDs, checking lists of credits, having a good rapport in the interview, and/or getting personal recommendations of others with whom he has worked.

If prescore is required, make sure that all musical and technical synch issues are thought through; consult with a composer or music editor weeks in advance of the shoot.

Communicating with the Composer (Chapter 3)

Trust the composer's professional abilities; listen to his suggestions. Don't overcontrol. He wants to give you the best score you've ever heard. Give him the tools necessary to do that. Give guidance, not instruction.

Meet frequently with the composer. Listen to music together so that you're able to define common dramatic/musical terminology and establish a musical direction.

The Rough Cut (Chapter 4)

Spend time with the composer screening scenes, discussing characters and dramatic points, listening to music, agreeing on general musical concepts. Experiment with playing CDs of film or concert music with scenes (preferably using only music that is possible to duplicate within your budget).

The composer can begin to work out rough themes and preview them for you on piano or synthesizer. Build your vocabulary of communication with the composer.

The composer may be able to assist with the temp music track.

The Spotting Session (Chapter 5)

The filmmaker, composer, and music editor screen the locked picture, making final decisions about the beginning and end of each music cue and the dramatic content thereof. The music editor retires to a computer and types up spotting notes and timing notes for the composer (this takes one to three days).

After the spotting session (now knowing the total number of minutes of music in the score), the filmmaker, composer, music supervisor, and music contractor meet to discuss budget realities, estimating the number of days of recording required, size of orchestra, size of studio, etc.

The musicians, orchestrators, copyists, recording studio, mixer, etc., are booked.

The Composing Process (Chapter 6)

After receiving timing notes from the music editor, and confirmation of the size of the musical ensemble, the composer begins to compose.

If creating an electronic score, the filmmaker may meet with the composer every few days to hear the finished cues. If creating an acoustic score, a few crucial cues may be previewed for the filmmaker. In this case, wait until the final recording session to make fine-tunings; at this point, just make sure that the composer is headed in proper general direction.

On average, the composer can only write two to three minutes of finished music per day *after* themes have been approved. Meetings with the filmmaker, previewing cues, etc., makes for less music being written per day. Find a reasonable balance.

If the score is orchestral, the composer sketches cues, which are then orchestrated. Fully orchestrated scores are delivered to music librarian/copyists so that individual instrumental parts can be hand-copied.

Try not to recut the film at this stage. It throws off timings and can wreak havoc all the way down the music production line.

Approximate time required to compose a score: four to six weeks for a feature film, two to three weeks for a television movie, seven to ten days for a one-hour television episode.

The Recording Session (Chapter 7)

The composer and the filmmaker should have learned necessary communication skills during rough-cut discussions to make efficient use of the recording session as they discuss and make alterations in the score. Play back the music cues with film, dialogue, and rough sound effects. This is the only time and the only way that the composer's musical vision can be accurately judged.

Plan on recording approximately three minutes of error-free music per hour; less for high-budget feature films, more for television episodic.

Composers, Orchestrators, Arrangers, Ghostwriters, Hummers, and Plagiarists (Chapter 8)

A composer is one who writes out or has complete knowledge and control of all the musical elements, such as note choices, tempo, orchestration, etc. In Hollywood, a composer generally writes out a short-hand sketch, which is given to an orchestrator.

An orchestrator assigns specific instruments to certain chords or melodic lines within the composer's sketch. Sketches from the best composers require only a cleaning up and expansion to a full orchestral score, from which the copyists may extract the individual instrumental parts.

Arranging usually involves more note choices than orchestration. It falls in the area between composing and orchestrating and involves working with a preexisting melody written by the film composer or making a new arrangement of a piece of music from the standard literature.

A ghostwriter is the real, unnamed, uncredited composer of the music because the composer of record is incapable of doing it himself due to laziness, greed, or lack of compositional craft. This costs the studio/production company more money than is necessary—one way or another, they're paying for that extra help of the ghostwriter when the "composer" is unable to perform his legitimate function.

The hummer has virtually no compositional craft, but merely hums (or plays one-finger piano) a melody that is then used by the real composer(s)/ghostwriter(s) to create the score.

A plagiarist, whether intentional or not, steals musical ideas from other sources and calls them his own. This is often a result of composers being fearful of deviating too far from the temp music track created (and loved) by the filmmaker.

The Music Supervisor (Chapter 9)

There are two basic categories of music supervisor: (1) the independent music supervisor who, for the most part, works on independent films, and (2) the studio music director, who oversees all music matters and administration on studio projects.

Their two main functions are to (1) facilitate logistical details and creative communication between composer and filmmaker and (2) help select songs and negotiate the deals with the publishers and record companies for the soundtrack.

The Music Editor (Chapter 10)

The music editor is crucial to the timing and synching of the music to the film. Although the music editor's role is not always visible to the filmmaker, trying to get by without hiring one is an enormous mistake.

The music editor helps with prescore situations, creates the temp track, attends spotting session, prepares spotting notes and timing notes so that the composer can write music to properly fit the film, prepares purchased songs for dub, prepares videotape or film with streamers and clix before the recording session, assists the composer at recording session with timing changes or writes down special instructions for prelay or dub, synchs up music tracks with film in preparation for dub, attends dub, and compiles cue sheets for production company to submit to ASCAP or BMI.

Use of Songs (Chapter 11)

There are two categories of songs that can be used in a film: (1) preexisting songs and (2) original songs written for the film. Preexisting songs need to be licensed for use in a film; it can be time consuming and expensive, so plan ahead. Hire an experienced music supervisor or clearance house to assist you.

ASCAP and BMI (Chapter 12)

ASCAP and BMI are performing rights societies. They collect fees from the venues that perform the music and disburse royalties to writers and publishers of music. ASCAP and BMI are *not* composers' unions.

Understanding the publishing and writing royalties of ASCAP and BMI can be helpful to production companies. If the production company offers a share of the publishing royalties to the composer (and lyricist if applicable), the composer will usually settle for less money up front.

Musicians' Union: American Federation of Musicians (Chapter 13)

On the whole, the union agreements have evolved over decades and are fair for both management and musicians. Although some money can be saved by scoring overseas or non-union domestically, it's often not worth the hassle once the expenses of airfare, hotels, per diem, the occasional lower caliber of musicians and recording studios, etc., are factored into the equation. Union musicians and studios in Los Angeles, New York, and London are still the most efficient, most versatile, most consistent in the world.

Package Deals (Chapter 14)

When contracted under a package deal, the composer receives "x" number of dollars, produces the entire film score, then hands the production company a finished master tape, pocketing as salary whatever is left over. Unless the score is done in a home-synthesizer studio, package deals are usually not a good idea because the composer spends too much time and energy on administrative matters, which takes away from composing.

Music Budgets (Chapter 15)

Many variables influence a music budget—most of which aren't even known until postproduction. The style of music, the instrumentation, the amount of music, number and types of songs to be purchased, etc., all play a huge role. However, a good general rule of thumb is that the music budget should be 1.5% to 2.5% of the total film budget.

Don't skimp on the music budget. Virtually every great film in history has a strong underscore, and that requires time and money.

Synthesized or Acoustic? (Chapter 16)

Usually not an either/or proposition. Even when a score is orchestral, most composers use a synthesizer as an added color. Synthesized music is best when conceived for synthesizer and not used to replace acoustic instruments.

Low-budget films do not automatically mean that an electronic score is necessary; clever film music can be written for a small ensemble of acoustic instruments (with perhaps a touch of synthesizer).

Unless used tastefully, synthesized music can make your film seem dated very quickly.

Final Thoughts (Chapter 17)

The production of a film score is an extremely complex process. Make sure that the composer has a reasonable amount of time, money, and good communication with you so that he may fulfill your creative vision.

APPENDIX 1
ADDRESSES

Partial list only—complete list and updates may be found in the *Hollywood Reporter*'s Film and TV Music Special Issue, which is published each January.

Society of Composers and Lyricists (SCL)
400 South Beverly Drive, Suite 214
Beverly Hills, CA 90212
(310) 281-2812

COMPOSER REPRESENTATION

Air Edel
1416 N. La Brea Ave.
Hollywood, CA 90028
(323) 802-1510

Blue Focus Management
15233 Ventura Blvd., Suite 200
Sherman Oaks, CA 91403
(818) 380-1919

Creative Artists Agency
9830 Wilshire Blvd.
Beverly Hills, CA 90210
(310) 288-4545

Carol Faith Agency
280 S. Beverly Drive, Suite 411
Beverly Hills, CA 90212
(310) 274-0776

The Gorfaine/Schwartz Agency
13245 Riverside Drive, Suite 450
Sherman Oaks, CA 91423
(818) 461-9600

Greenspan Artists Management
6777 Hollywood Blvd.
Los Angeles, CA 90028
(323) 468-1450

Ingenuity Entertainment
9000 Sunset Blvd.
Suite 300
West Hollywood, CA 90069
(310) 247-4324

Seth Kaplan Entertainment
8440 Santa Monica Blvd.
Suite 202
West Hollywood, CA 90069
(323) 848-3700

The Kordek Agency
211 W. Alameda Ave.
Suite 101
Burbank, CA 91502
(818) 526-1626

Robert Light Agency
6404 Wilshire Blvd.
Suite 900
Los Angeles, CA 90048
(323) 651-1777

William Morris Agency
1 William Morris Place
Beverly Hills, CA 90212
(310) 859-4000

Derek Power Co.
818 N. Doheny Dr.
Suite 1003
Los Angeles, CA 90069
(310) 550-0770

SMC Artists
4400 Coldwater Canyon
Suite 127
Studio City, CA 91604-1480
(818) 505-9600

Soundtrack Music Associatesß
8938 Keith Ave.
West Hollywood, CA 90069
(323) 724-5600

PERFORMING RIGHTS SOCIETIES: ASCAP, BMI, SESAC

ASCAP (LA)
7920 Sunset Blvd.
3rd Floor
Los Angeles, CA 90046
(323) 883-1000

ASCAP (NY)
1 Lincoln Plaza
New York, NY 10023
(212) 621-6000

BMI (LA)
8730 Sunset Blvd.
3rd Floor
Los Angeles, CA 90069
(310) 659-9109

BMI (NY)
320 W. 57th Street
New York, NY 10019
(212) 621-6000

SESAC (NY)
421 W. 54th Street
New York, NY 10019
(212) 586-3450

All of these societies have major offices in Nashville

MUSIC CLEARANCE COMPANIES

BZ/Rights and Permissions, Inc.
125 W. 72nd Street
New York, NY 10023
(212) 580-0615

Copyright Music & Visuals
67 Portland Street
1st Floor
Toronto, Ontario
Canada M5V 2M9
(416) 979-3333

Diamond Time Ltd.
73 Spring Street
Suite 504
New York, NY 10012
(212) 274-1006

Essex Entertainment, Inc.
144 Second Avenue North
Suite 150
Nashville, TN 37201
(615) 244-9305

Arlene Fishbach Enterprises
1223 Wilshire Blvd.
Suite 304
Santa Monica, CA 90403
(310) 451-5916

Harry Fox Agency
711 Third Avenue
8th Floor
New York, NY 10017
(212) 834-0102

Fricon Entertainment Co., Inc.
1048 S. Ogden Drive
Los Angeles, CA 90019
(323) 931-7323

Evan Greenspan, Inc.
11846 Ventura Blvd.
Suite 140
Studio City, CA 91604
(818) 762-9656

Media Musiconsultants
10669 Santa Monica Blvd.
Los Angeles, CA 90025
(310) 441-2604

Diane Prentice Music Clearance
8720 Woodley Ave.
Suite 232
North Hills, CA 91343
(818) 830-1270

Screen Music International
18034 Ventura Blvd.
Suite 450
Encino, CA 91316
(818) 789-2954

Signature Sound, Inc.
71 W. 23rd St.
Suite 902
New York, NY 10010
(212) 989-0011

The Winogradsky Co.
12408 Magnolia Blvd.
Suite 104
North Hollywood, CA 91601
(818) 761-6906

APPENDIX II
RECOMMENDED READING

On the Track, Fred Karlin and Rayburn Wright, Schirmer Books, 1990.

> With over 600 pages of text and examples, this is the definitive book about filmscoring. Although much of the information is geared toward composers, myriad interviews and quotes from famous producers, directors, and composers give excellent insight into the collaborative process of creating a film score.

Listening to Movies, Fred Karlin, Schirmer Books, 1994.

> An invaluable book for the film buff and filmmaker, it describes the process of creating a score, provides a close study of eight famous films and their scores, includes an overview of the evolution of film music, a list of composers and their credits, soundtrack information, filmography and bibliography. As in *On the Track*, I find the numerous quotations from composers and filmmakers to be just as illuminating as Karlin's concise text.

Knowing the Score: Notes on Film Music, Irwin Bazelon, Arco Publishing, 1975.

> Although hard to find because it's out of print, this book is excellent for all students of film. Beginning with a short history of film music and its function, the major scope of the book is extensive interviews with famous film composers as they relate their experiences working with various filmmakers over the years.

No Minor Chords, Andre Previn, originally published in hardcover by Doubleday in 1992, paperback edition published by Bantam in 1993.

> Also difficult to find, but an extremely witty and insightful look back on Previn's career as a film composer from 1946 to 1975. Full of delightful anecdotes about Hollywood's inner workings at that time.

* * *

The following are excellent resources for information about performing rights societies, contract points, royalties, fee information, attorneys, agents, business managers, distribution deals, copyrights, licensing.

Music, Money and Success, Todd Brabec and Jeff Brabec, Schirmer Books, 1994.

All You Need to Know About the Music Business, Donald S. Passman, Prentice Hall Press, 1991.

The Art of Music Licensing, Al Kohn, Prentice Hall Press, 1992.

GLOSSARY

CARTAGE. Costs incurred when large instrumental equipment (synthesizers, percussion, harp, etc.) is delivered and set up by a cartage truck and crew prior to a recording session. After the recording session, the crew breaks down the equipment, packs it into shipping trunks, then returns it to a warehouse or storage in the musician's home.

CLICKS or **CLIX**. Generated by a digital metronome or computer, these repetitive ticks are fed to the musicians' headphones so that they are better able to play with precision. Clix are usually used for music that requires a steady beat such as chase music.

CUE. Each piece of music within the film is labeled a music cue, or "cue" for short.

CUE SHEET. When the score is dubbed into the picture, the music editor makes a list of all music cues (purchased or original), their length, their use, their writers and publishers. This is sent to ASCAP, BMI, and SESAC by the production company or studio so that proper royalties may be distributed.

DOUBLE (INSTRUMENTAL DOUBLE). A "double" occurs when a musician is proficient on more than one instrument and is asked to play that second or third (or fourth, fifth, sixth, etc.) instrument during the same recording session in which he is using his primary instrument. For instance, when a flute player also plays a piccolo or alto flute in a few passages written by the composer, he will get 50% in addition to base scale for that second instrument; another 20% in addition to base scale will be added to that if a third and subsequent instruments are called for. Other common "doublers": synthesists with multiple keyboards or acoustic piano, trumpet players doubling flugelhorn or high trumpets (such as piccolo trumpet), reed players who play several instruments (clarinet, bass clarinet, alto sax, tenor sax, etc.), percussionists who play several instruments, guitarists who play both acoustic and electric, etc.

MASTER USE LICENSE. This allows you to use the original artist's recordings of a preexisting work and is negotiated with the record company who owns the master tapes. This can be the same amount of money as the synch fee. Not only must the record company receive their fee, but all of the artists on the recording must receive repayment of their original union wage for reuse (in current dollars). The record company is responsible for this, which is included in their fee. This holds true whether the recording is a single artist playing a piano solo or an entire orchestra—each musician gets repaid.

MIDI. The acronym for Musical Instrument Digital Interface, this is the electronic language that allows synthesizers, computers, and electronic musical instruments to talk to one another.

MUSIC CONTRACTOR. When the total amount of music to be recorded is known, the music contractor assists in figuring the size of orchestra that will fit the budget. He then consults with the composer and books the necessary musicians for the recording date. During the recording session, the music contractor, although a member of the musicians' union, acts as a referee, ensuring that the musicians are given proper breaks and pay but also protecting the production company from overcharges. The music contractor can be an enormous help to the filmmaker in getting the biggest bang for the buck.

MUSIC LIBRARIAN. Usually the supervising music copyist, the music librarian makes sure that all instrumental parts are copied from the score, organized into "books" (folders) for each musician, writes out orchestra breakdown for each music cue so that the recording session can be planned most efficiently around diminishing numbers of musicians, transports the parts to the scoring session, passes them out, and makes corrections or changes on instrumental parts during recording session if music score is substantially altered. This person can estimate copying costs, access studio score libraries for source music, and take care of myriad other details relating to session.

MUSIC SOUND CONSULTANT. Known by a couple of titles (booth supervisor or music sound consultant), this person sits in the recording booth next to the scoring mixer with a set of scores and helps cue the scoring mixer for solos or other musical events necessary to get the mix right. Usually, this person has also orchestrated the music for the composer and is very familiar with the musical concept.

NEW USE PAYMENTS. "New use" payments are owed to union musicians when a recording is used in another category or production. For instance, if a cut from a record album/CD is used in a film or television show, the musicians must be re-paid 100% of their salaries from the original recording session (in dollars of current television scale).

PACKAGE DEAL. The "package deal" composer contract became prevalent in the mid-1980s and is generally considered by many composers to be most workable when the score is com-pletely electronic and done in the composer's home studio. It's used in most television productions, some medium-bud-get films and virtually all low-budget films. In the package deal, a composer is given a set amount of money and is re-sponsible for the administering, producing, accounting, and composing of the music score. He receives "x" number of dollars, then hands the production company a finished mas-ter tape at the end of the scoring process, pocketing whatever is left over as his salary.

PRESCORE or **PRERECORD**. Music that is recorded before the shoot. This is necessary when actors or dancers need to synch singing, dancing, or playing an instrument to a particular piece of music.

SCORING MIXER. The scoring mixer operates the mixing board to ensure that the instruments are in proper balance and equal-ization with one another. He also oversees the operation of all recording equipment and proper microphone placement around the musical instruments.

SOURCE MUSIC. This is the music that emanates from a source on screen; it is usually a radio or a performing music ensemble.

Unless the actors are seen singing, playing, or dancing in synch to the music, this is added during postproduction. It can be a piece of preexisting music that's purchased for the scene or something composed and recorded by the film's composer.

SPOTTING NOTES. During the spotting session, the music editor makes spotting notes (see Example 1), which are the footage numbers at the beginning and ending of each cue. While making the spotting notes, the music editor assigns each cue a number (m11 or 1m1 means first reel, first music cue; m12 or 1m2 means first reel, second music cue; and so on).

STREAMERS. A streamer is an almost-vertical line that takes three seconds to pass from the left side of the screen to the right, ending with a small burst of light, a "hole-punch." On film, where the end of the streamer occurs (the exact frame to be synched), a standard office hole-punch is used to make a hole in the film, which causes a flash of light to appear when projected on the screen (computers generate a similar flash on videotape). The streamers serve as synching cues for the conductor and music editor. Generally, a yellow streamer signals for the warning clix to begin (a certain number of warning clix is specified by the composer so that the orchestra will hear a few beats of the proper tempo in their headphones before they actually begin to play). A green streamer signals the actual beginning of the cue, white or blue streamers (which have various meanings) are interior signals within the music cue, and a red streamer signals the end of the music cue. Drawing or computer-generating the streamers on film or videotape can take the music editor one to three days, depending on the complexity of the score. As the composer completes cues, the streamer information is relayed to the music editor (by the music librarians who have picked up the composer's finished orchestra scores or the composer's computer, depending on the way the composer works); he then draws the streamers on the film with a scribe and colored markers or with computer graphics if he's working on videotape.

SUPPLEMENTAL MARKET PAYMENTS. "Supplemental market" payments are owed to union musicians when the project is sold to another market (i.e., feature film to video, television movie to feature distribution, feature film to airlines, etc.).

Whatever entity owns the project (production company or studio/distributor) and receives income from a backend sale will owe the AFM 1.5% of adjusted gross (approximately 60% of actual gross) from that sale. The AFM distributes this money to the musicians who played the recording sessions for that soundtrack.

SWEETENING. Adding instrumental tracks to a foundation of synthesizer and/or rhythm tracks already on tape.

SYNCHRONIZATION LICENSE. The "synch license" allows using the sheet music of a preexisting work in the film and is negotiated with the publisher(s) of the song. This grants the rights to arrange/record your own version of the work, not use any preexisting recordings (see "master use license" for these rights). The identity of the publisher can be gotten from the record, CD, or sheet music. It's necessary to contact the publisher (this is usually done by the music clearance department of the studio/production company or an independent music clearance company) and describe the use of the song within the film; i.e., the length of the use, the context within the scene, how prominent (coming from a radio in the background or being sung on screen by an actor in a featured performance). The price will vary, depending on whether you want a big hit song or a "throwaway" (a lesser-known cut by the same artist). The prices for the synch license can range from a few dollars for a song you purchase from your nephew's rock band to $200,000 for a current hit.

TEMP TRACK or **TEMP MUSIC TRACK**. For the purposes of screening the unfinished film to studio executives or test audiences, filmmakers usually employ a music editor to construct a temporary music soundtrack using music from other films. This is also used to communicate the filmmaker's musical intentions for the final music score. Having the composer help construct the temp track is a good way for the composer and filmmaker to communicate general musical concepts for the final score.

TIMING NOTES. After the spotting session, the music editor retires to a moviola (or video/computer setup) and types up the timing notes, a detailed and accurate list of timings of each event within the music cue (see Example 2). The composer must have these exact timings so that he can weave the music into the scene, making the proper mathematical/musical calculations for hitting or missing certain events in the film. The music editor is able to begin work only after a copy of the locked picture is delivered to him, and then it will take approximately two or three days for the timing notes to be completed and delivered to the composer so that he may begin writing.